LUMINOUS LIFE:
A New Model Of Humanistic Psychotherapy

Partha Choudhury

CW00551584

Copyright © 2011 Partha Choudhury

Library of Congress Cataloging-in-Publication Data

Choudhury, Partha
Luminous Life: A New Model of Humanistic Psychotheraphy
p.cm.
Includes bibliographic references.
      1. Psychology - Humanistic. 2. Psychotheraphy.
      3. Personal Transformation. 4. Health - Psychotheraphy.

ISBN 13: 978-0-9820467-7

Bäuu Press
PO Box 1945
Winter Park, CO 80482

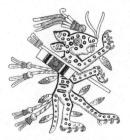

Printed in the United States of America
All Rights Reserved

Dedication

Babi, Pampa, Nikhil and Swamyji

Acknowledgement

Many people have inspired, encouraged, supported and blessed me towards the writing of this book. I thank them all; Pampa and Nikhil, my late father and my mother, my brother's family, my mother's sister's family and my in-laws; my patients and clients, their families and friends; all the institutions I have trained and worked in; NIMHANS in particular, where this therapy was originally developed; all of my teachers, colleagues and students; humanistic-existential traditions in psychology and all psychotherapies; my spiritual benefactors: Late Rangama, Late Jnananandaji Maharaj, Late Atmanandaji Maharaj, Late Nemai Chand Goswami, Late Shivaswamy, Mrs. Jaya Ramachandran, Mr. Satish Suri, Pandit Hemendra Nath Chakrabarti; my friends: Sayantan-Sagarika-Byjayanti, Adrish-Roma-Shreya, Ashish-Late Bijay Maitra-Mashima-Ashok, Yogesh and Mridula, Raghav and Vidya, Amitava, Bimalendu, Mohit, Sougata, Sanjay Verma, Harish Sinha, Amites and Anindita, Nileen, Prabha Chandra, Venkatasubramanian, Sanjib Sinha, Satyajit, Partha Basu, Swapan Kumar Ghosh, Amalendu and Shukla De, Arunodaya and Vrunda, Rajesh Sagar, Neena, Shyamoshree Sinharoy, Jyothi and Shaji, Prabudh and Nirupama, Giridhar, Heide, Anneke, Dave, Aniruddha Deb, Jaydeep Sarkar, Mike Nair, Keith Bickley, Trevor Keith, Sanjay Gehlot, Sandip and Suchitra, Madan Gopal Goswami, Debashish Chakraborty, Gerdje Van Hoecke, Debabrata Chatterjee and Jana Raychoudhury, Sugata Sarkar, Ramkrishna Das, Shubhankar Roy...; those well-wishers who are no more on this earth but whose love continues to enrich my life; Prasad and Venkatesh of Nagasri; Mr Chakrapani; my solicitors; Varanasi, Bangalore and Carlisle and last but not least my God.

I have been immensely benefitted by the ancient Indian Sanskrit texts that I have quoted from the books: Isa Upanisad and Manjul-Manjusha (a compilation of renowned Sanskrit texts); my heartfelt thanks to their authors/publishers.

My sincere thanks go to my publishers The BAUU Press.

Many more names of my friends and benefactors should have been mentioned here but could not be mentioned because of a shortage of space.

The magnitude of my indebtedness is staggering. Not even an iota of this debt is repayable, ever. I am glad to remain indebted, ad infinitum.

Partha Choudhury
February, 2011

TABLE OF CONTENTS

Introduction

The book derives its name from an ancient Indian philosophical concept: 'Atmadeepo Bhava'. Human life is essentially a solitary activity, although it is often seen and understood in the context of other people and situations.

If you see around you during your hours of need, do you find anybody else? You do not. You only encounter yourself, a lonely sufferer, who has to walk alone to complete her journey. Then who do you have for help, to fall back on? It is none other than you. Who shows you the path, tells you what to do? It's you again. This is the understanding of 'Atmadeepo Bhava', which literally means 'Be your own light'. In other words, be your own 'Friend, philosopher and guide' on your life's journey.

This is not to minimize the contribution of the important others or the world at large. Neither is it to undermine the presence and participation of God in your life. This is merely your affirmation of faith in you as a human being. This is an attempt to establish you as a person who is capable of looking after yourself when the need arises. Once you become your own light, the path of life is illuminated. Your life becomes luminous and stays that way. You not only become healthy and strong but also happy and helpful towards others.

The feminine gender has been used deliberately to represent both genders including the references to God throughout this book.

I have tried to present a new model of humanistic psychotherapy in this book. These understandings developed over nearly a decade while I was involved with the treatment and management of different mental health problems. The aim of this book is to document those understandings systematically and to present them in a format of 'Self-Help'.

The theoretical constructs did not develop suddenly or even over a short period. They started to crystallize when I started as a consultant at NIMHANS (National Institute of Mental Health and Neuro Sciences India), working actively in psychotherapy with difficult cases, particularly those with personality disorders. While doing the therapy these therapeutic concepts started growing and evolving. As I conducted several hundred hours of individual psychotherapy the 5

theory gradually expanded and the modules became differentiated. It took a while for me to realize that these concepts could
be put together as a model of humanistic psychotherapy.

Alongside discussing theory here, I have attempted to
include some practical aspects of this psychotherapy. I, my family and friends and my clients have tried and found many of these
practices beneficial.

All humanistic psychotherapy in essence is self-therapy.
It is the person who wants to change herself, makes the changes
herself. This is also true for the therapy this book is about.

This therapy attempts to deal with the person and her
meanings and motivations in life. It offers a set of major modules and a few additional modules about the theory. Suggested
practices are linked to both types of modules.

These modules are seemingly independent but essentially linked. Together they offer you a system of working with
yourself, trying to solve the problems and aiming to grow as a
person. The modules can be used in isolation or in conjunction
with one another. You are free to choose which aspects of the
theory to dwell on or which practical methods to follow.

I have been undoubtedly influenced by the stalwarts of
this field: Frankl (1970), Maslow (1987), Surya (1993) and Rogers (2004). Of course my formal training in psychiatry and in
psychotherapy as well as life's teaching has helped me.

This book is about understanding and changing the
myriad processes that constitute your life. These processes are
both within and without you. The past has a bearing on your
present. Present is the time when you act. The future is when the
results happen. Therefore the emphasis is on 'here and now'; on
how you understand your life situations and your problems, and
finally on how you can change your condition.

These concepts are primarily humanistic though a certain overlap with some existential concepts is both understand-
able and unavoidable. I have quoted some ancient Indian texts
in Sanskrit along with my translations (aided by the published
translations and by Pampa).

'Luminous Life' has so far been used for adult individual
therapy with the exception of a few cases of family counselling.
It has the scope for being used as promotive and
preventive therapy. A wider application, including   6

couple's, family, and group work and work with special populations remains to be made.

There is one request. If you are a professional counsellor or psychotherapist, please seek my written consent before using any material of this book in any of your professional therapeutic work. You are free to use the materials of this book for yourself, both the theory and the practices.

The credit of this work, if any, goes to everybody and everything that has helped towards it. Whatever the shortcomings, they are mine.

Humanistic Approach To Mental Health Problems

In Luminous Life, mental health is seen as a sensitive indicator of the overall quality and completeness of human life. If you feel that certain things are not working, or others strongly feel the same about you, then acknowledge it first. As usual the first step is the most difficult. Being introspective and taking a pro-health stance are the next moves. The more harmonious the different components of life are, for example work, leisure, personal things, family, friends, interests and commitments, the higher the mental well-being becomes.

In this book the emphasis is on promotive and preventive mental health. We are not talking about severe mental illnesses here. For those problems one should seek expert help from a mental health team.

Mental health problems have been understood in diverse ways using different theoretical perspectives. There are three major approaches.

The psychodynamic understanding makes use of the principles of psychoanalysis in which the issues of childhood development, as well as repressed memories, are addressed. The repressed material is manifested as anxiety, depression and other mental symptoms which are treated by establishing the connection between the past and the present.

The cognitive-behavioural understanding makes use of various learning theories in which faulty learning and behaviour are addressed. Life's adverse experiences generate illogical thinking which produces the symptoms of depressive as well as anxious thoughts. In order to treat those symptoms, the negative thoughts are recorded and then replaced by neutral and positive thoughts. Alongside this the maladaptive behaviour is modified.

In the existential-humanistic approach towards mental health the major emphasis is on the realities of life and its potentials. The primary focus is on how we ascribe meanings to our actions, how we try to actualize our potentials, how we execute our choices and take responsibility for them. Mental health is affected when we move away from or deny these important questions. The person attempts to find answers to these questions in therapy.

9

These schools of thought have been developed into major psychotherapies. They are perhaps more complementary than in conflict with one-another.

Human life remains an enigma. It is understandably influenced by the past; both by the personal life-story as well as the collective history of humankind. It is obviously influenced by the particular situation of an individual and the multiple aspects of the modern world. Also our aspirations are projected in the future.

Whenever there is a lack of harmony among the various aspects of health; wherever there is a lack of balance between loving self and loving others, there is a disproportionate stress that may lead to mental health problems. If there is a large reservoir of negative emotions inside, it is difficult to feel at ease. In a similar way if the connections are few and far between for someone, she is likely to remain isolated and to an extent, insecure.

If the will power is low, she may remain stuck with her old and unhealthy habits. If the relationships are the difficult area for the person, her life is usually not trouble-free. If the family is over-involved and critical, it often leads to an atmosphere of conflicts and confrontations. And if there is dissonance between the values of the individual and those of the prevailing culture, it gives rise to tension and dissatisfaction.

When 'time' is not handled well or 'negotiation' is not the preferred mode of dealing with the world – when 'creativity' is inhibited and when the individual does not appreciate her benefactors – her well being is hampered in the long run.

There can be further inquiries into these issues. Specific humanistic formulations on the genesis and development of anxiety, depression and several other mental health problems may be discussed further. However, this is a self-help book and the detailed discussions are out of its scope.

Major Modules

Health: A Holistic Consideration

It is now well known that health and well being are not limited to the field of physical health. Many experts, including the World Health Organization (WHO) mention the mental and the social health as necessary constituents of complete health. Also religious/spiritual health is now being recognized as an important part.

It must be said that today we know a good deal about the causation, course and treatment of many physical disorders. In comparison, we still know a lot less in the field of mental health, even though we have made tremendous progress in the past hundred years or so in this field.

While approaching the area of social health we realize that we know even less. It is not known exactly what kinds of social relationships are conducive to which aspects of positive mental health. We do appreciate the value of the supportive family and social networks though.

Philosophical and cultural aspects are the areas that directly affect health but our understanding of them is even more limited. Recently we have started recognizing the important roles of these different influences.

A six-sided model of health is therefore suggested. Apart from the already established physical, mental and social aspects, I include three more: cultural, material and lastly spiritual.

This model is to be conceptualized like a 'cube' having six interconnected sides or to use a more familiar analogy: a 'room'. A conventional room has four walls, one floor and one roof. The last two constituents are absolutely necessary but the walls are also needed. If any one wall were removed, the room would change into a lounge; if two were taken away, it would become a corridor; and if three were got rid of, the room would be reduced to a porch. In any case it would cease to be a room where it would be comfortable to live in.

Therefore a full set of four walls and in effect all six surfaces are mandatory for a healthy system. Curiously, material health may be thought of as the floor that supports

11

the walls and spiritual health the roof that provides a canopy for all other aspects of health.

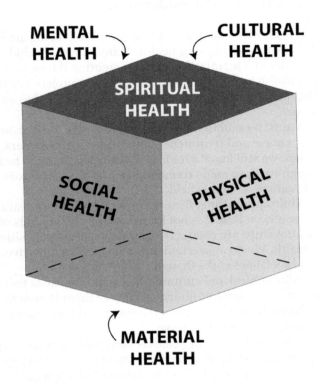

Philosophical health could theoretically claim a seventh wall but I suggest that it should be thought of not as a separate wall but rather as the atmosphere of the room. Without a sound philosophy of life it would become futile to talk about health.

An amount of positive input into any one aspect of health should bring about positive changes, albeit small, in the other aspects. Nonetheless it is important to focus on the individual aspects. I would urge you to be more aware of all aspects of your health and to try to bring as much life and harmony into each one as possible.

Mental health is not covered separately in this section since the whole book is about it. Mental health problems are quite common and will be talked about in brief. They affect all age groups and are present in all countries and cultures. Most mental illnesses are understood as multifactor in origin – Nature and Nurture both playing their important roles. Many of these illnesses can now be managed to a reasonable extent with the available knowledge, skill and resources.

The misconceptions and the stigma attached to mental health problems are constantly being fought the world over and they are improving gradually.

Mental health problems require a multidisciplinary team approach for their successful management including ongoing care. Psychiatrists, psychologists, nurses, social workers, occupational therapists and various other professional people together form these teams. A detailed mental health assessment by a trained person is often a useful starting point. Medicines are essential interventions for many mental illnesses as are the different kinds of counselling and psychotherapy. Rehabilitation in various walks of life is as important as the care for the condition.

We shall now consider the elaborations of the rest of the aspects of health.

Physical Health

A few important points for enhancing physical health would be:

Exercise:
Your overall level of physical activity is perhaps the most important factor in keeping your body fit. The less sedentary your lifestyle is the less will be the need for additional exercises. There are various kinds of exercises and all have their specific merits. Aerobics, i.e., walking, jogging or running burn calories & keep body weight in the normal range. They also keep your heart healthy. Weight training builds muscle mass that helps you to burn calories more efficiently and keeps you in shape. Stretching exercises keep the body flexible. Relaxation exercises keep the level of stress down. Yogic 'Asanas' and other procedures are known to bring about a harmony among the various organ systems of the body and keep them healthy.

Taking part in various sports and athletic activities is really useful. If you are already a sportsperson, keep it up! If you are not, maybe it is not too late to pick up one.

You would do well to follow a regime that has inputs from different kinds of exercises and that is easy to start and maintain. Discontinuation is a major problem. You should not lose heart if you stop, simply start again from where you had left off. Even a little exercise is infinitely better than none at all. Whenever you are in doubt please consult an expert, for example, a trainer.

Diet:
What you eat is important. Contradictory opinions keep on appearing in the media and it can be frustrating at times to be able to decide on the right diet.

Fortunately some guidelines have withstood the test of time. They include:

1. Eat a variety of natural, organic and whole foods, like fruits, salads, seeds and nuts including raw preparations like sprouts. Seasonal and local produce are very important;

2. Drink plenty of water and juices;

3. Avoid high-fat, high-salt, high-sugar and an excess of processed foods;

4. Avoid over-eating, under-eating and irregular eating such as snacking;

5. Eat light, balanced and frequent meals; try to have a harmonious mix of all major categories of nutrients: carbohydrates, protein, fat, vitamins and minerals.

6. Keep the intake of animal products limited, including the meats;

7. Occasional fasting within the 'comfort zone' is practiced by some people. It helps to cleanse the system.

You would need to choose your own pattern as well as the ingredients, to continue to eat and drink in a healthy way.

Rest:
Different people have different requirements for sleep. It is useful to find out what your pattern is; how many hours of sleep you need. Missing on nights sleep once in a while may be all right, but it should not happen on a regular basis. Sleep deprivation is a risk factor for many mental health problems.
You would do well to learn about 'Sleep Hygiene' to get the best benefit from your naturally occurring sleep.

Alcohol, Tobacco and Psychoactive Substances:
All psychoactive substances if used should be used judiciously and carefully. Some social usage is common and perhaps unavoidable sometimes. It is important to keep your consumption occasional, moderate and under control.
There are a few words of caution necessary for any safe substance use. If you notice that there   16

is a persistent increase in either the frequency or the amount of consumption, it would be prudent to cut down your usage pattern. If your individual efforts do not suffice, seek help from family and friends. If that too doesn't help, consult the professionals or other specialized help.

Please remember, accepting that you have a substance use problem is often the most difficult part and always the starting point for recovery.

Health Monitoring:

Periodic health check-ups are advisable in your middle years and afterwards. Even when you have no appreciable symptoms of ill-health, it is necessary. Silent disorders such as high blood pressure and diabetes are often not detected otherwise.

It is best to consult your doctor who knows you and your bodily systems well. The same should be done if you develop any symptom (for example, cough, pain and wounds) that tends to persist for a long time or does not improve with everyday measures. This would help in the early diagnosis and treatment of potentially serious diseases.

Sexual health:

This is one area that is rife with controversies. It is truly multifaceted and multifactor. There are numerous historical and cultural influences as much as the debates about the rights and the wrongs.

Two healthy minds in two healthy bodies engaging in a specific healthy and loving relationship should ideally constitute the sexual health for those two adult people. The relationship is important in the act of intimacy. Also, safe sex is indispensable.

It is vital to control the temptations and greed in this area perhaps more than anywhere else in life. Greed is discussed at length in the section of 'Self'.

Alternative sexuality is a reality and should always be dealt with sensitively, honestly and with respect.

You as an individual should treat this aspect of your health with utmost care. If your life is balanced and harmonious you are likely to have a healthy sexuality.

Social Health

The social dimension of health can not be overemphasized. We perhaps do not fully appreciate how important it is. In fact it is the social aspect of life that primarily differentiates the human beings from the other advanced primates. Human social life is elaborate and complex. It is multi-level, multi-stage and multi-purpose.

Your life is socially embedded. You are a daughter to your parents, a sister to your siblings, a friend to your friends, a partner in your intimate relationship; in short, you are in a different role with different people. You are an individual and are in relationships with many people, all at once. All these roles are being enacted parallel and simultaneously. The essence of social health lies in harmonizing your relationships, one with the other.

Your existence as a social being remains a truth even when you are walking alone on a crowded street or working alone in an empty office.

You are also part of a larger group of people, the society. In any situation you are governed by its rules and conventions and are contributing towards them. There is also scope for healthy dissent and disapproval for anti-social behaviour.

Your family is your immediate society and remains with you at an emotional level even when you are physically separated from them and interacting with the larger society. In the family you sometimes have to share your life with people who are significantly senior or junior to you. Your relationship with someone like your parents is bound to be different from that with your partner, which in turn will be different from that with your child.

Everybody is at a different station of life. It is important to recognize this fact and to adjust your relationship with each individual member according to their specific positions. Each individual as well as you has her own agenda, own strengths and weaknesses. Your needs and those of the others require you to be coordinated with one-another. Know those needs, help others and get helped in return. This approach works well for the family as well as for close friends.

Spending quality time with people is important; particularly with children and elders. It is a good practice to allocate specific time slots; for example, for discussing the news headlines with your father and for playing rough-and-tumble with your child. You would do well to reserve one slot for chatting up with your friends and another for romancing your partner.

Networking with people is important, especially in today's ever-changing world. You should build up the connections with like-minded people who share your interests and concerns. The examples could be joining a club of fitness enthusiasts or a society of amateur anglers. A book club is a good idea and so is a musical group. Not only will you develop a circle of friends, but you will also be fulfilled in many other ways.

Helping others is a great way of becoming socially active and healthy. Altruism is one of the most useful qualities and voluntarism is a major social development. You can start voluntary work anytime and anywhere. There are always useful things to be done; whether it is raising money for a hospice, finding foster care for disturbed children or spending quality time with the inmates of a care home for the elderly. If you are interested, look around. You will find at least some ways to influence the others' lives in a positive way.

Of course the social ethos affects its citizens greatly. The more just and friendly a social group is the more honest and loving its members are going to be and vice-versa. It is a two-way process. But the beneficial influence of a network of positive-thinking individuals may not be apparent until a critical number of them have been reached.

Social needs are numerous and so are the ways of responding to them. The civic side of social life is also important, which essentially means following the rules and the major conventions.

Obeying the law, for example, maintaining the traffic rules should become a compulsion rather than a choice. Accidents and traffic jams would be greatly avoided if everybody followed them properly.

Following the conventions, for example, maintaining a queue is essential. A lot of time can be saved as well as the convenience ensured if the queue system is adhered to.

You as a citizen are the keeper of laws and

conventions; it is not the government alone. In fact, you could take an active interest in governance, starting with your locality. Try to follow government procedures. Look for transparency and accountability. Build up a system of give-and-take. If at all possible, choose honest and hard-working people to run the posts. Good governance is the cornerstone of a social structure and is best handled at the local level.

Cultural Health

This aspect of health is becoming more important than ever. We are all cultural beings as much as we are social. We are born and raised in certain cultural traditions and live our adult lives amid a great cultural diversity. There are influences from the traditional cultures, the modern ones and the numerous 'fusion' cultures.

You are aware of and responsive to the various cultural options. It is something like a buffet spread in a restaurant. The choices of dresses and accessories, books and movies, norms and lifestyles are indeed like the multitude of soups and salads and entrees and desserts. This spread is available all the time, in nearly all corners of the world, thanks to the advent of the global media and the internet.

The space in your stomach and on your plate is limited. So is your capacity to try out and assimilate the different cultural ingredients. Hence there is a pressing need of a specific cultural formulation for the particular individual that you are. If you know what you like as well as what is good for you, there will be less chances of going wrong. Once your formulation becomes stable, you will be able to choose right most of the time; no matter where you are or how variable the spread is. To the extent you are able to choose wisely, to enjoy your selection and to benefit from it, you are deemed culturally healthy.

There is a tendency of a globally dominant culture taking over the individual preferences and making our lives largely uniform and one-dimensional. There are strong dictates on what to wear, eat, drink; how to work, enjoy leisure, date; possibly also how to think, feel and have a particular attitude.

We have known the benefits of multi-cultural living that have survived over thousands of years across different civilizations. Therefore it is better to refuse to be a passive recipient of the global cultural onslaught and to strive to become a free-willed culturally participating individual.

Exercise your choice and build up a cultural repertoire that is rich and varied; carefully selecting the particular ingredients from different cultures of the world. Your choice of working dress may be modern Western; the leisure-time attire may belong to the Caribbean. Your favourite art   23 may be French Impressionism; the favoured music South Indian Classical. Your preferred beverage may be coffee from Columbia and the choice of food Far Eastern. Your favourite writer may be J.L. Borges and the admired poet Rabindranath Tagore. The combinations could be endless and that is precisely the point. Your cultural formulation should be as unique and individualized as you are. Your chances of thriving in a rapidly changing world will vastly increase if you are culturally aware and active.

There are multiple sources for forming cultural affiliations. You have to choose your sources carefully. Here are a few suggestions.

The printed medium has the benefits of being easy-to-use and keep and relatively inexpensive. Literature is one of the most outstanding as well as one of the most enduring expressions of human mind. The writings in different languages and even those in the same language across different cultures have distinct substances and flavours. Reading can be nurtured into a healthy habit. You can pause, think, reflect, generate your own ideas and have discussions with others.

Start reading: fiction, non-fiction, anything you like. The wider and more varied your reading, the more areas of interest that will open up for you. Like other cultural choices, you will gradually develop a list of books to become your lasting companions. You can read them again at variable intervals.

Apart from reading about your everyday culture, I would suggest writings from different countries and cultures; particularly contemporary fiction and non-fiction. They make you acquainted with the aspects of the modern world that are different from your own. Another suggestion would be for reading the folk literature alongside the classics.

Music is another area to cultivate. Not for nothing it has been called 'divine' and a 'fair gift from God'. Every place has its own music: traditional and modern, folk and classical, vocal and instrumental, solo and chorus. One gets spoilt for choice.

World Cinema is a great treasure house of creation too. Movies often reflect the subtle nuances of human life. A truly uplifting movie lingers in your memory for a long time.

The electronic media are by far the most assertive, sometimes even aggressive. Excessive viewing of the satellite TV, as practiced in many households, is 24 largely a passive experience of enjoyment. Usually it is the serials or the sports, often in mega dose, and at the expense of most other kinds of pleasurable activities. It tends to limit your capacity of exercising the mind.

Excessive indulgence in video and computer games usually over-stimulates you but affects you in a similar way. An element of control is necessary about these kinds of cultural activities.

Live performances are few of the 'real' pleasures of life. Singing, dancing, miming, reciting a poem, telling a story, staging a play; all these activities involve the artists and the audience in a unique way. Most cultures that are close to Nature have rich traditions of live performances. I recommend them wholeheartedly at the conclusion of this section.

Material Health

The material aspect of health is not talked about much, possibly because many are uncomfortable with the idea. Actually one's material situation often determines the status of one's health.

If you are not comfortable materially, all aspects of your health are likely to suffer. If you can not live in clean and less polluted surroundings and can not consume wholesome and hygienic food and drink, your physical health is likely to go down. If you are continually worried about economic security, your mind will not remain healthy for long. Your social health will also suffer, if you are not able to adequately spend time in everyday give-and-take social networks. In a similar way your cultural health will be in jeopardy, if you have to think twice before spending at each cultural celebration.

Only the spiritual and the philosophical aspects of your health will possibly not be affected by your material situation, but one can not be too sure of that. Most of the time if you are busy fighting your poor material conditions, your philosophical system may also lose its robustness or your spirituality its shine. In essence, material health is the foundation on which stands the edifice of all other aspects of health put together.

We know of members of a loving family turning into fierce critics of one-another at some stage of their economic hardship. At a further level of penury they become bitter enemies or the unfortunate competitors for life's meagre resources. Life can be terrible if the material conditions remain poor over a long time and love may simply not be enough to make it otherwise. For people living in chronic poverty there is not much meaning left in life, let alone its beauty and transcendence.

The idea is to be materially sound and comfortable. It is not only about your economic status but also about the management of your money, your overall resourcefulness. Four methods of improving the material health are suggested here.

The first method is called 'Application', which is about focusing on your remunerative work. Whether a paid job or a business or vocations like farming; whether part or full-time; you will have to engage fully. You will need to be committed, punctual and hard-working. Take pride   27 in and enjoy your work as much as possible. Not everybody is fortunate to get her dream job, but it is still essential to do well whatever you are supposed to be doing. The stress of the job is real and job stress and job satisfaction are often inversely correlated. One has to apply herself, nonetheless.

The second is called 'Moderation' and is about cutting down on spending. Try not to have very expensive food very frequently. For example, out of a possible fourteen main meals in a week, try to eat five times frugally, five times moderately well and four times lavishly. This will not only save money but will improve your physical health in a major way. Another example may be an attempt to reorganize your wardrobe. All twelve pairs of dresses need not be very costly. You may choose to have four pairs of everyday wear, five pairs of moderately costly dresses and three pairs of designer ones.

It is always a good practice to save up money for spending rather than taking out a loan straightaway. For certain major expenditures (e.g. buying a house) or for immediate requirements (e.g. getting a car or a computer) a loan may be necessary. The same can not always be said for the holidays or for shopping. The idea of going for a bigger loan to pay off the smaller ones is not a bright idea; at least not for you, who will have to repay the loan eventually. The prevalent culture of debt is not a healthy one.

The third one is called 'Caring'. It is important to take good care of the material possessions if they are to serve us well. Timely repairs are necessary for your home; regular servicing is essential for your vehicle and periodic upgrading is valuable for your computer.

The fourth method is called 'Sharing'. Car pooling is a good example. Pooling a vehicle among five persons, travelling between the same areas for work purposes, actually provides multiple benefits. If managed well, it would mean, each day only one vehicle out of five is on the road. It cuts down the cost of fuel, as well as traffic and parking loads, and of course pollution. It would also mean a one-in-five rota of driving responsibilities, cutting down the stress of driving. Such an arrangement is also likely to further better social relationships among the sharers.

You can think of many other ways of sharing resources. Of course it can happen only among   28 trusted and like-minded friends and relatives. Whatever you do not need for your everyday personal use, it can potentially be shared with these significant others. I can suggest still and video cameras, tents and other outdoor equipment and even books and DVDs. Needless to say you will have to bring down your level of possessiveness about your things for such sharing to happen. Others too will have to be careful while sharing your things.

All these methods will not only save you money but will also make you a better manager of your resources.

Philosophical Health

Philosophical health is the environment of the 'room' in the six-sided model of health described above. It may also become the supportive canopy for those who do not believe in spirituality.

It is important for you to have a coherent and stable philosophical system. An awareness of the existing values and the world-views is useful. Also an honest attempt towards attaining a set of values is important. These values should encompass the personal as well as the impersonal aspects of life and provide you with a ready frame of reference. This system is something that you would have developed and acquired from many sources over the years of your growth, and that you can call your own.

A philosophy worth adhering to has to be a forward-thinking, optimistic, broad-minded and positive one. It would probably be a pro-Nature, pro-life, pro-human, and pro-social philosophy. It should embolden you to face life as it is; enrich you to enjoy it; and empower you to change what needs to be changed. It should teach you how to live best. It's your life and it is a single life after all.

In formulating any structure anywhere, keeping an open mind is a must. Whenever a duality, that is, a 'fork' situation appears, acknowledge it first and then try to make a conscious choice. Many people surrender or connect to The Universal Consciousness at a 'fork' situation and allow the energies to take the best course. The level of surrender or connectivity again depends on the individual. The structure you build could be anything depending on your level of consciousness, but let it not be rigid; keep it open and flexible when the need arises. Human experiences tell us that 'trials' do come. Let it be a progressive, ongoing system.

There are other bits of defeatist, divisive, alienating, and pessimistic points of view that may be continuously vying for your attention. In today's highly differentiated and complex socio-cultural scenario, it is quite possible to get swayed sometimes by these negative approaches. One has to be on guard.

Spiritual Health

If you are a non-believer, I respect your choice. This aspect of health will not be of interest to you.

Spiritual health is being increasingly recognized as an integral component of holistic health. Religiosity, as well as spirituality-related mental health problems has been frequently mentioned in recent years. As a reflection of that, the 'Religious or Spiritual Problem' has been included as a category in a major system of classification for mental disorders, the DSM-4 (American Psychiatric Association 1994).

Religiosity is adhering to the practices of an organized religion. All religions have a lot of commonality in spite of their outward differences. They have nurtured and supported humankind across time and cultures and deserve respect for the positive values they uphold.

Spirituality is an issue that encompasses the bodies of all religions yet remains larger than the sum of all of them. 'God', 'The Great Spirit', 'The Supreme Being' – there are many different names for the same concept. Spirituality states that God is the essence of everything existing in the universe. The ancient Indian text describes it as:

*"Sah paryagāt śukram akāyam avranam
Asnāviram śuddham apāpaviddham
Kavih manisi paribhūh svayambhūh
Yāthātathyatah arthān vyadadhāt śāśvatibhyah
samābhyah"*

*'He is all-pervasive, pure and bright, bodiless, without wounds, without sinews, taintless, untouched by sin, omniscient, ruler of mind, transcendent and self-existent. He has dually allotted the respective duties to the eternal years
(that is to everything).'*

(Isa Upanisad: 8; Gambhirananda 2000)

The closest glimpse I get from the above verses is that of Pure Consciousness. The Sanskrit description of this is 'Saccidanand (Sat-Cit-Anand)', which can be   33 broadly translated as 'Existence-absolute; Knowledge-absolute; Bliss-absolute'.

Spirituality affirms that an intimate relationship with God is real and possible now and always.

Spiritual health also includes a set of philosophical understandings and human values that can be summarized as an essential commitment to all life, human and non-human. Different religions have talked about them in their commandments. It speaks of positive thoughts, feelings and attitudes that are pro-Nature, pro-life, pro-human and pro-social.

Believing in God and trying to reach God is one and the same thing; amalgamated in an activity called 'Prayer'. Prayer is one of the most direct forms of establishing a connection with Her. Time, energy and effort-wise, it is cost-effective.

Prayer is one of the nodal activities around which a person's spirituality may grow. Try to pray everyday: consciously, deliberately, and of course, lovingly. Let the prayer permeate your life; shower you with the blessings every moment.

It is a good idea to build a personal prayer. You can shape it the way you like. Remember to pray for yourself as well as for the others including your near and dear ones. It is important to pray for everybody.

> *"Sarvastaratu durgāni, sarvo bhadrāni paśyatu*
> *Sarvah kāmānavāpnotu, sarvah sarvatra nandatu"*

> *'May all overcome their obstacles. May all see prosperity. May all have their wishes fulfilled. May all be happy everywhere.'*

> *(Vikramorvasiya/5/39; Manjul-Manjusha: 1482)*

It is useful to pray separately for your short-term (e.g. brief illness) and long-term requirements (e.g. education of the children). Praying should include your local needs (e.g. fine weather) as well as the global ones (e.g. Global warming). There should also be separate slots for the personal (e.g. success in romance) and the impersonal prayers (e.g. win for your favourite team). Don't forget to thank God and to wish Her well.

34

Asking for forgiveness may be a part of the prayer or it could be a separate exercise. Yet another aspect may be praying for the departed souls including all your ancestors. Praying for the betterment of Humankind and the future of the earth could also be included.

We, or in fact the whole universe, is created and nurtured by the Supreme Consciousness. This in other words is 'Life': all-encompassing. There are four separate yet overlapping aspects of nurturance. A close simulation of such nurturance can be found in what a parent usually does in order to successfully raise a child. Not for nothing God is addressed as the 'Father' or the 'Mother' in most religions.

You will notice that the same four activities are essential if you wish to care for your own self or for the others. Therefore, they can be considered the essential aspects of nurturance under four major headings. Curiously the names of all four aspects start with 'P': Providing, Protecting, Problem Solving and Personal Teaching (hence The Four 'P's).

Providing: A parent provides for her children everything that is required and that is within her reach. The list of provisions may range from every day food, clothing and shelter to education, values and culture. I believe that God does the same thing for Her children, that She is a provider par excellence. The provider aspect of various religious shrines and many famous saints is well-known.

Protecting: A parent attempts to protect her children from all possible dangers to the best of her ability. Such a protection may range from teaching the child not to play with fire to teaching her to handle the traffic carefully and to arranging the necessary money and the logistic support for future expenses and possible emergencies. God too keeps on protecting us from countless dangers, both everyday and the major ones. The concept of the 'Protector Saints' is known in many countries.

Problem Solving: A parent tries helping her children solve their own problems. If they can not, she herself tries to solve their problems. Either way her role is pre-eminent as children are hardly equipped to handle all problems on their own. God too helps us to solve our problems and to help us avoid troubles. This aspect of divine intervention in problem-solving is known in several cultures.

Personal teaching: A parent is essentially a private tutor for her children; teaching them life's necessary skills for survival and growth, how they should develop and branch out in their lives. This teaching is specific and general, local and global, immediate and long-term at the same time. In short, such training is tailor-made for the pupil. God also teaches Her people the same way; helping them to grow as individuals and to fulfil their potentialities. This aspect establishes the belief that God is the source of all knowledge and wisdom.

If I reflect and try to understand how exactly my parents and my God have worked so far, sometimes in tandem, to shape what I have become today; I realize that it has been a personal and individualized training, leading to my overall knowledge and skill.

These four activities function together in God's work as they do in parenting. You could ask for each of these aspects in your prayer.

Also consider that your life's script is written jointly by you and God. Life is a joint venture. Since childhood it has been a script that is written in collaboration between you and Her. As you grew up your participation became stronger. As you strive to go along the path of a Luminous Life; your contribution will become even more prominent, because you will be walking essentially alongside your God.

Forgiveness

Many of my clients have had significant negative experiences during their years of growing up. Those included neglect as well as abuse . Emotional abuse was the commonest, followed by physical and also sexual. The impact of these traumas is usually long-lasting. It makes a person vulnerable for future mental health problems of various kinds. The factors commonly associated with the traumatized clients include inconsistent parenting, chaotic home atmosphere and the lack of protective care-giving. A few people are of course resilient – they have no major problems in spite of having had similar trauma in childhood.

All of us have a reservoir of emotions inside us. A large part of it consists of negative emotions: anger, fear, sadness, etc. Anger is something that lasts for a long time residing deep within. A part of this anger is directed towards others. Another, possibly larger, part is directed towards the self, being presented as Guilt. It is difficult to get rid of all this anger. It dissipates slowly, if at all.

People tend to hurt one-another wittingly and unwittingly. This happens day after day, sometimes throughout life, by various acts of commission and omission. Memories of such hurts – emotional, physical and sometimes sexual – stay with us and within us for many years. You need to get rid of those painful memories, to cleanse yourself from the damaging twin emotions: anger and guilt.

The common wisdom 'Forget and Forgive' needs to be turned on its head if it has to be effective. It should be 'Forgive and (then) Forget'. You can not forget unless and until you have overcome the hurts, in other words 'forgiven'. The smouldering emotions need to be put out, the poisonous memories rendered harmless.

It is definitely easier said than done. Saying something like 'I forgive you for the hurt you gave me' is not easy at all. It is even more difficult to tell yourself the same words.

A way of saying these difficult words is suggested. It is in the form of a prayer. The non-believers are free to omit all references to God and make the 'prayer' a 'declaration'. It should work nonetheless.

All forgiving has to be unconditional. There can be no expectations of change in the person if you have to forgive someone completely (of course the damages should be strictly in the past and not ongoing). If you attach any strings, it will never succeed. Leave aside others; you may not be able to meet your own expectations; and as a result the forgiving will not happen.

A realization of the wrongs that you have done either to others or to you has to be there at the back of your mind along with a stand of repentance; before you start asking for forgiveness. This will be your preparation that is indispensable for the process of forgiving.

Put this prayer in a place (written/printed/on-screen) where you can visit it at will. Read it at least once a day and if you feel up to it, several times.

Forgiveness Prayer/Declaration:

> *"I realize that others have hurt me on many occasions. I realize that I too have hurt myself many times. I want to forgive others as well as myself unconditionally, for all the hurts and wrongdoings.*
>
> *I understand that I have hurt others on many occasions. I understand that others too have hurt themselves as well as the others in a similar way. I wish others could forgive me and themselves unconditionally, for everything.*
>
> *I know that forgiving somebody unconditionally is one of the most difficult things to do. Our sense of righteousness, shame and pride, all oppose it. Also we love our hurts too much and do not want to part with the painful memories. I pray to God to give me and the others the necessary courage and strength to forgive.*
>
> *I also pray for myself and others to be forgiven unconditionally, for all the wrongs we have done."*

That is it. Once you try, you will know how difficult it is, to read through these lines. But it is worth the trouble. Read them and repeat the words in your mind. Just pay a 'lip-service' to start with. Slowly, with every passing day, the words will start having an effect on you. Slowly your resistance to engage in forgiving will diminish. Gradually the hurt and anger within you will dissolve.

Once you have achieved a level of mastery in this process, feel free to add the details of your personal life. You may choose to add the descriptions of the hurts; the details of the insults and injuries that you are trying to forgive.

Speak out the name of the wrong-doer, your own name too, if that is the case. Describe the offence. Narrate the story in some detail. Do all this entirely within your zone of comfort. There is no need to overdo things. Do not bring in any details if you do not want to. Go only till the point at which you can withstand the bitterness as well as the anger that might suddenly well up. Then ask for the forgiveness.

You may not get the desired results quickly. The massive reservoir of pain within will appear to remain unchanging for a long time. But you will find yourself a little less resentful everyday, a little stronger, possibly a little happier. As you will realize, forgiving somebody is an ongoing process and not an end-point. It is truer for your own self than for anybody else.

Forgiveness is not easy. Seeking retaliation or frank revenge is actually much easier. Forgiving is one of the highest and rarest human attributes. It has also been hailed as such:

"Narasyābharanam rūpam rūpasyābharanam gunah
Gunasyābharanam jñānam jñānasyābharanam
ksamā"

'Man's beauty is handsomeness of his body; virtues
are the beauty of the handsome body; knowledge is
the beauty of the virtues and forgiveness is the beauty
of knowledge.'

(Narabharana/2; Manjul-Manjusha: 843)

Self

'I' in my case and 'You' in yours: each one of us is our
own 'Inner self'; in other words, 'The person' inside a person.
The self is the 'core' of the being. The term 'self' is used in this
book to describe the sum total of the psychological apparatus
and its functioning. It contains a person's all inner tendencies,
all values, all likes and dislikes. Self in this sense has been used
to replace other similar and overlapping terms such as 'Ego',
'Psyche' and 'Mind'.

Self therefore comprises thinking, feeling, perceiving
and all other psychological functions. The closest analogy will
be that of the 'Body,' which is the sum total of the physical apparatus. Thus what body is in relation to physical health, self is
in relation to mental health. The module of self includes 3 sub-
modules:

1. 'Self' and 'Others': two distinct entities

As each individual's body is different from that of anyone else; same way the self of each person is distinct in comparison with one-another. In fact it is one's unique and individualis-
tic self that distinguishes her as a person from the rest.

Your self is a unit, independent and complete. The way
your body does not have to be rooted to a particular place is the
same way your self is separate from everybody and everything
else. Your life is not a part, shadow or reflection of anyone else's
life. You exist in this world as a free and distinct entity.

There are of course your family, close relatives and
friends, other kin and acquaintances, colleagues and neighbours.
Also there is the large group of humankind and even larger
groups of animals, plants and micro-organisms. Also Nature exists as a whole, including the material world.

You and all these are separate. You are different from
everything else; everything else is different from you. Everybody's life's origin, development, course and culmination are
different from those of yours.

This mass of everybody and everything is called: the
'others', individually or collectively. In all discussions about your
self, the 'self' is you. These two entities are separate

41

and distinct. This is the first major concept regarding self.

What does this concept mean to you? It means that your self governs your life and the others' selves govern theirs. You are primarily responsible for your growth and well-being and the others are for theirs. In many societies and many families this distinction is not emphasized and therefore not respected. Rather there is over-involvement and to a great extent, 'vicarious living'. Those tendencies are not conducive to the healthy growth that an individual should normally expect. You should try to live your life as fully as possible and so should others. You must let the others live their lives as much as they must let you live yours.

You are an adult. All that has happened in your life during the growing years, you were responsible for some part of that, even though others were responsible for the larger part. For all that is happening to you now, you are responsible almost as much as others are. For whatever is going to happen to you in the future, your share of the responsibility is going to be larger than that of the others. As you grow older you make more conscious choices and thereby take more control over your own life. At least that should happen normally, barring illnesses, accidents, or any other exigency.

In many situations, determined by the prevalent scenario or by the demands of your own individual life, you are not in a position to make conscious choices all the time. Therefore the balance between the relative responsibilities of you and the others may not always progress in the way described above. Nevertheless, each person's life is and should be largely governed by her informed and conscious choices.

Of course you do not want your choice to be inferior in quality. So you need to differentiate between the wants and the needs. For example, you may not want to have safe sex but you need to, every time. Try to make the choices that make your life more effective and increase happiness.

According to the theories one can say that troubled childhood causes so many things. But in reality, it is seen that different people cope with similar situations in very different ways.

As a final word, it is your life and you always have some choice at any given moment. If you are looking for a   42
change in your life, the world is not going to change

for you. You have to make that shift within you. To do this, use all available resources, seek help and above all work for your well being.

When working with your self, the distinction between the self and the others should be borne in mind. Though these two are independent they are also connected and often inter-dependent, as we shall see in the module of 'Connections'.

2. 'Loving self and loving others': two inseparable concepts

What usually happens is like this. Either you are very concerned about your own well-being or you are neglecting it a great deal. In a similar way you are either neglecting others too much or you are caring for them excessively.

In case you are caring for yourself too much and have been doing that for long, you will probably become a selfish person. Being selfish is not very compatible with your eventual growth as a person. Consider the following.

Your average day starts with an overt exercise of making yourself presentable to the world. Most of the working hours are spent in pursuing your personal ambitions of fame and fortune. Most of your evening is spent either in work spill-over or in the acts of self-indulgence, like watching TV endlessly or drinking. Where is the scope of your growth?

In case you have been caring for others excessively and that too for a long time, you are likely to become an out and out altruist. An inordinate amount of love for others usually leads to a relative neglect for your own self and its well-being. Consider the following.

You are so preoccupied with taking care of others in the morning that getting ready yourself takes a backseat. At work you are too busy helping others than minding your own business. In the evening you are trying to help others at the cost of your rest and leisure. Where is the scope of your well-being?

In either of these two extreme situations, you as a person have suffered. The balance between the two is therefore crucial for healthy growth of the self and also for a healthy relationship of the self with others.

How does one go about achieving this? You get the answer when you consider 'loving self' and   43 'loving others' are intimately related. There can be no separate 'head' or 'tail' sides of a coin. Neither can there be two separate sides of a credit card, one bearing the number and the other the magnetic strip. The twin concepts of 'loving self' and 'loving others' are inseparable in exactly the same way.

One could say, perhaps for the sake of argument, that you can use a fine-toothed saw to cut through the fused entity such as the coin or the credit card. The point is, even if such a thing was done, the entity would no longer remain a coin or a credit card. It would merely become two separate surfaces that would be useless for financial transactions.

There is a saying; 'If you don't learn to love yourself, you can not love others'. 'Loving self' and 'loving others' together is a complete and balanced functional unit, ready for a process of 'give and take' with the world. This approach should therefore be your preferred currency when you deal with your life.

A balance does not mean that it has to be a fifty-fifty division all the time. Sometimes when you are unwell, you need to take rest and receive care. Sometimes when a near one is ill, you need to help her get well. The demands of a particular situation will guide you how to bring in the balance between these two tendencies. I presume you already have a balance working for you. I merely ask you to be more aware of it and to try to improve the balance as much as possible.

One of the best ways of 'loving self' is by taking good care of oneself. You should feel responsible for your overall well-being. Trying to improve your appearance through grooming and dressing is an example. Keeping your living quarters clean and tidy and maintaining your workstations uncluttered and efficient are other examples. Similarly, keeping your vehicles in good running conditions may be seen as a favour that you do to yourself. Yet another example would include taking care of the different aspects of your health.

All these efforts if put in for others should enhance the overall love for others.

You may wonder whether you are actually taking good care of yourself or not. If you are doing reasonably well in most areas of life perhaps this level of care is all right.

Whether you are taking good care of people around you is a more difficult question. You may get   44 to know partly by observation and partly by asking. Neither of these methods in isolation is fully satisfactory.

Consider the following as a more or less balanced day for you: You get up somewhat early in the morning so as to have enough time for a brief workout, for getting ready and for helping your family to be ready for the day. This help could be anything: making beds, fixing breakfast or sending the little ones off to school. At work, you concentrate on your own work but also manage to find out how your colleagues are doing and to assist them a little if needed. This assistance can again be anything: discussing a point, sending a mail or making a phone call on someone's behalf. In the evening, apart from making preparations for the next days work and winding up the day along with your family, you try to find a little time for something extra. Try to do a little of something that is special to you and a little of something that is special to someone else. Two such examples could be: listening to some music you like or giving quality time to your child and watching the happiness in her eyes. You of course need to find the separate slots for intimacy with your partner and for your prayers.

This design usually serves well for a typical workday. 'Loving self and loving others' need really to be interwoven with each-other. There could be somewhat different but essentially similar routines for your weekends and brief holidays.

Longer vacations may be different altogether as would be the periods of additional stress, for example, illness, etc. Whether you should take more care of yourself or of the others would then depend on so many different factors.

This is a stand that helps in living in a balanced and harmonious way. For you, who want to change her life for the better, it should be useful.

3. *Pro-self and anti-self: two opposing components*
One of the pioneers of humanistic psychology Abraham Maslow has described a 'hierarchy of needs' (Maslow 1987). He suggested that human needs could be organized in the form of a pyramid. The tiers of this pyramid (from below upwards) are: 'biological needs (hunger, thirst, etc.)'; 'security needs'; 'belongingness needs'; 'growth needs (creativity, etc.)' and 'self-actualization needs'.

45

The construct I suggest here is related to the higher motives. Self can be understood so as to have two contradicting tendencies: 'pro-self' and 'anti-self'. These tendencies have always been present and they operate simultaneously. All those attitudes and actions of an individual that help the 'self' towards achieving its growth motives are the 'Pro-self' system and all those that oppose the fulfilment of the growth motives are the 'Anti-self' system.

For example, developing healthy habits like exercising or learning to relax on a regular basis would be the work of your pro-self system. Significant self-indulgence in either alcohol or computer games would be the work of your anti-self system.

Pro-self and anti-self are forever in conflict with each-other. No one can enhance all pro-self or eliminate all anti-self any more than one can really make oneself either an angel or a demon. This opposing dual system is a part of the human existence, as fundamental and as unavoidable. The idea is to be aware of the two systems and to try to achieve a positive balance towards the pro-self.

Elaborating on the anti-self system, we see that there have been allusions to this area in various cultural and religious texts. In ancient Indian texts we read about the 'Shada-Ripu' or the 'Six Enemies'. These 'enemies' are the obstacles that a person progressing on the spiritual path faces. They are 'Kama (Lust)', 'Krodha (Anger)', 'Lobha (Greed)', 'Moha (Attachment)', 'Mada (Pride)' and 'Matsarya (Envy)'.

Curiously these 'Six enemies' are very similar to the 'Seven deadly sins' described in Christianity: Lust, Anger, Greed, Pride, Envy, Gluttony and Sloth.

These six vices could be understood as the different manifestations of a single negative human quality and that is greed. Greed indeed is the common denominator. Lust can be understood as 'Greed for unbridled desire' and Anger as 'Greed for forceful dominance over others or for righteousness'. Attachment can be understood as 'Extended greed'; Pride as 'Greed for self-importance' and Envy as 'Greed for other people's possessions and qualities'.

Greed has always been one of the central negative tendencies of human beings and is perhaps the most powerful one. It has been the major motivation in   46 the expansion of various empires. From the Romans to the Mongols to different Nations trying to conquer others, there has been overriding greed with them all. In the modern world we see an extraordinary growth and development of greed both at the individual and at the societal levels.

It can perhaps be expanded like this: "I want the best material things, power and control for me and my group. It does not matter to me whether the others get any of these benefits at all." These thoughts are present in our minds on a regular basis but we are always not aware of them. They are the motivational basis for the exploitation of other human beings, other living beings and of Nature as such.

Poorly controlled greed is everybody's problem. It often leads to the other vices as mentioned above.

"Lobhah pratisthā pāpasya, prasūtirlobha eva ca
Dvesakrodhādijanako lobhah pāpasya kāranam"

'Greed causes inception of sin; greed indeed generates enmity and anger etc; greed is the root of sin.'

(Bhojaprabandha/1; Manjul-Manjusha: 1260)

You would do well to control your own greed and so would anybody else. There are no readymade or even easy solutions. There are no permanent or even long-term

remedies. Neither is there a premium in today's world on any attempts to keep one's greed under control.

Can you see the major manifestations of your greed? Is it an indulgence in good food and beverages? Is it a craving for fine dresses and shoes? Is it a preoccupation with promotion and power? Is it a tendency to dominate in the intimate relationship? It could be any or all of these. Or it could be some other manifestation.

Once you have got a lead —say it is the food or the drink— you should make an attempt to quantify it. Keeping a diary of the intake is difficult but very useful. At the end of a period, say a week, you become more aware of what all and how much you have been eating or drinking. Then comes the crucial part of decision making. You have to decide what part of this intake is your actual bodily need, how much more is required for your mental satisfaction and what amount is really the excessive indulgence. Then you should try to chip away at the indulgence deliberately and slowly.

An example would be reducing the number of your everyday scoops of ice cream from four to two and then two to one. After that you should handle the 'mental satisfaction' bit. Is it really necessary for you to have a little ice cream everyday to keep you happy? How about having it two or three times a week? If this becomes feasible, the logical step would be to try to make it once a week. You will need to be flexible and at times generous towards yourself. If you reach the stage of having an ice cream once every week, then the intake can be increased from one to two scoops. Instead of carrying the guilt everyday you can enjoy these two scoops guilt-free.

Please do not deprive yourself totally. Rather try to find a workable balance.

You should also make sure that you are not replacing one bit of indulgence by another; for example, not eating chocolates in excess to compensate for the reduction in the intake of ice cream. You will require very careful negotiations with yourself to reduce the consumption any further.

Actually, the body needs no ice cream to remain healthy. It would take you a long and arduous process to move to a situation where you eat an ice cream only occasionally. Also by that time you would have learned other ways to satisfy yourself, than with your favourite foods.

This may sound like over-simplification but it is not. The method described above is called 'Controlling the Greed'. How much and how exactly is left to your own motivation and judgment. Start humbly and move gradually towards controlling it.

I chose a simple and rather exaggerated scenario to describe the process. Obviously for a different manifestation of your greed, such as 'manipulating the office milieu for your promotion-related gains,' would need a similar but much more detailed approach. You would probably need the support of a good friend to help you see the complexities of such a problem and to overcome it slowly.

Controlling your greed is more of an attitude rather than a particular attempt or even a set of attempts. You can never rid yourself of all greed

48

because it will amount to eliminating your anti-self. Controlling too is possible only after a lot of sustained effort.

The following story highlights how I learned about finding a new balance between my whims and needs. It also led to a negotiation between my needs and those of others'.

Up until recently my holidays to my home country used to be very stressful. I nearly always visited many places within the country, far away from one another, that required much time and effort. I have a pronounced greed of 'Being good to people, being close to them'. I always met a long list of people, who all were very important to me and tried to spend some time with each one of them. I always ended up feeling tired, hassled and extremely dissatisfied. To make matters worse, I dragged my family along, whose priorities were clearly different from mine. Understandably they were unhappier than I was.

Then a friend told the story about the recent visit to her native place. Earlier she would have a holiday similar to mine, if somewhat less hectic, but tiring and dissatisfying nonetheless. But she had discussed this with her family and planned to visit less number of people and spend more time together as a family instead. They strictly followed the new plan. They informed a few people about their program and did not worry too much if they could not meet somebody. As a result their latest visit was more relaxing and fulfilling than earlier. After returning she wrote letters to those friends and relatives whom she could not meet.

I too had known where my problem was and what the solution would be. I lacked the initiative to bring about the change. My friend's story inspired me to do similar things in my visit that followed their's. And it worked out for me for the first time in life!

This time too it was hectic, but slightly less so. I followed one major lead and that was meeting fewer friends and relatives. I still went to visit quite a few, but kept it under reasonable control. I prioritised who I wished to meet most. I was able to meet people on more than one or two occasions. I spent more quality time, went out for long hours and ate unhurried meals with them. I could have real talks with them instead of just exchanging pleasantries and then rushing off to another place. I felt less stressed than usual, simply because   49

I met a smaller number of people. My family too was less hassled.

I should not claim that I have learned the lesson yet. This was my first attempt at something new. If I stick to this pattern over many holidays and continue to benefit, then perhaps it will become one of my effective coping methods.

Another method could be to keep no timetable as far as practicable. If you don't chase a schedule, but do what you want to at a given point of time, you may end up doing more. Don't keep anything incomplete though. Suppose you have two aunts who are twins and you are okay with both, please make sure either you visit both of them or none. Whenever you have a dilemma, accept it and make a choice. Use your discretion, self, inner being, experience or whatever is tangible to you. Try to make a conscious choice as far as possible; too many loose threads left unattended do not allow your system to stay stress-free.

It is vital to at least try to keep a check on your greed. It is essential for the growth of your humane values, for example, tolerance, compassion, etc. There are certain approaches that are both available to you and practicable. 'Santosh' or 'Contentment' is an understanding that works as an antithesis of uncontrolled greed. It is achievable even for the person whose life is largely governed by greed. Developing contentment is an active process. But an amount of transcendence is necessary either through the spiritual advancement or through the philosophical reformulation.

At times you need to pause in your relentless pursuit of a cause and take stock. See if you are getting enough contentment from life's different aspects: work, leisure, family, socialization and everything that is important to you. Such stock-taking exercises need to be done on a periodic basis, every time cross-sectionally. You choose the extent and the intervals at which you wish to do them. Along with checking the things that are important to you, make sure that there is an element of contentment present at each stock-taking. If you can restore the harmony among the different aspects of life, the level of contentment is likely to increase. Contentment is not all or none.

Let your life's journey be depicted by a series of successive arrows spanning time and each cross-sectional stock-taking exercise be shown as the disc intersect-   50 ing this chain of arrows. Such exercises will give you a deeper insight about how your life is going.

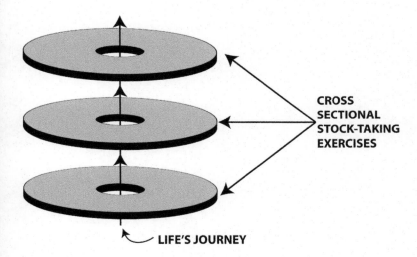

CROSS
SECTIONAL
STOCK-TAKING
EXERCISES

LIFE'S JOURNEY

I wish to conclude the module on the 'self' on a simple note. 'Self' is your 'core', your inner being. The more you are aware of it and the more you want it to remain healthy and growing, the better off you are going to be.

Connections

There are certain times when you feel lonely and isolated from others. On such moments you may feel there is no one to share a thought or a feeling. This may happen even when you are among people. At other times you are indeed alone and feel understandably bad about it.

The modern person is largely isolated from her fellow beings, her surroundings and the world. She considers herself self-made and rather self-sufficient. Such a strong stand is un-called for. All human life, indeed all existence, is perhaps inter-connected.

I had a young client who had taught me many of the basics of this entire therapy. He was an extra-ordinary individual, powerful and very sensitive. His primary issue was 'not having a meaning in life'. In everyday life there were adjustment problems with the parents, a passive lifestyle and a pervasive lack of motivation about studies or jobs.

We were together in individual therapy for many months. There were long periods of non-improvement, sometimes with virtual stalemates. But we persevered and after long, arduous and painful deliberations we were able to reach some common ground. He was finally ready to accept that there could be some meaning in trying to help some of the neediest people.

He could finally 'connect' to an issue and through that was able to find some kind of a 'meaning' in life. Though he did not actually start helping anyone; it was one of the turning points in the therapy from where he began his eventual journey towards wellbeing. Of course that required another long process.

Connectedness means a commitment to the connections that should exist for a particular individual if she wants them to exist. No connection exists 'a priori' in this sense. What is important is to realize a connection between you and others. Neither you nor they are alone. You know about the ties that connect people together; blood, marriage, kinship. There are further ties of friendships and acquaintances. And there are many others as yet undefined.

Think of yourself at the centre of many concentric circles, each one representing a group of people. The circle closest to you is of your immediate family   53 and close friends. The one just outside it includes your relatives, other friends and acquaintances. Still outer circles would consist of colleagues, neighbours and other people known to you. If you continue to proceed outwards you may consider yourself connected with many social, economic and cultural groups. They may be based on language, region, ethnicity, religion, cultural affiliation and so forth.

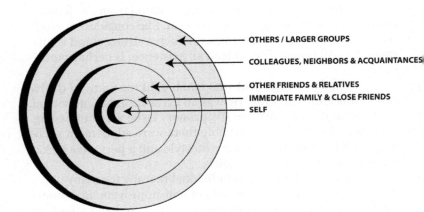

At a higher plane you may consider yourself connected to humankind as such, to animals, to plants, to Nature itself and indeed to all matter, energy, time and space!

Ancient Indian texts speak about connectedness in the following way:

"Ayam nijah paro veti ganana laghucetāsam
Udāracaritānāntu vasudhaiva kutumbakam"

'This is mine and that is theirs, calculating like this is out of lower level of consciousness. Entire world is the family for the broadminded.'

(Pancatantra/Aparikshitakarakam/35; Manjul-Manjusha: 114)

For the believers the task becomes easy. They are able to connect to the Supreme Consciousness in one form or the other. One of the easiest ways to connect is   54 through prayer; ask blessings for you, ask blessings for the others.

The act of connecting to anybody can be done by two methods. If a mode of communication exists and you are using that, then the connection would be direct, for example, writing a note, sending an e-mail or making a phone call to somebody. This method would be akin to a land-line connection.

The other method would be indirect, when you pray for somebody. You are still communicating your feelings albeit not in a direct way. When you are praying you are essentially asking God for the well-being of that person. Such a prayer could be for health, wealth, wisdom, long life, etc. Your prayer is directed to God and the resultant blessing comes from Her that reaches your target person. This method of communication operates through a relay station, in this case God. This would be akin to a mobile connection in which the satellite relays the message.

Forgiving, well-wishing, loving others, taking responsibility for your actions and repentance; all these can be done silently and will help you to come to terms with the people and issues already existing in your inner world. Gradually, you also learn to resolve the present using similar considerations and do not leave the painful or the unfinished issues.

Establishing connections is about strengthening the existing relationships and forging new relationships with things that are bigger, stronger and longer-lasting than you. The idea is to go from being small to being large, from being weak to being strong and from being transitory to being permanent. This realization should first be at a level of thought and emotion and only later at a level of commitment and action.

Everyone does not need to organise a charity or run a race to help the next person on the street. But the awareness towards being connected may lead you to act in a humane way in a 'here and now' situation.

Connectedness in this sense is a conscious deliberation and has a positive connotation. One can remain an individual while remaining connected to everyone and everything else in much the same way as a bucketful of water that is still inside a river. Such a body of water belongs to the bucket but also does so to every other particle of water starting from the origin of the river to its confluence with the sea.   55

There can be several exercises to strengthen existing connections or to form new ones.

Connect to your 'Self,' first. You are a composite of all your attributes, positive and negative. The combination is definitely unique even though few of the constituents really are. There is as yet no replica of a human being, the threats of 'cloning' notwithstanding!

You should be more aware of this individuality in your everyday life. Your height, physique, posture, gait, speech, smile, scowl, appetite, thirst and sexuality, all bear your personal stamp.

Perhaps at the present time you are able to accept some parts of yourself; you barely tolerate others and some you simply loathe. It is another thing that you like yourself for what you are in your totality. It would be even better if you could love yourself for your uniqueness.

Making a list of things that you already know and like about you helps:

How fit is your body? How fine is your mind? How distinctly do you dress? How is your speech? What are your eating and drinking preferences? What are your favourite books, music, sports, other hobbies? Who are the people you look up to? How personal is your everyday prayer? How personalized is your lovemaking? What are your very own working habits? How unique are your leisure activities?

Pondering over these questions will make you more aware of yourself than you already are. Trying to solve some of your everyday problems and praying for your own 'self', will further secure the connections.

Develop a system of feeling and expressing the gratitude for your everyday life. Tidy up your living room and feel the joys of the cosy surroundings. Enjoy a quiet evening and thank your room, sofa, TV and other things. Similarly lay the table carefully and settle down for a nice meal. Thank your food and drink and feel nourished. Keep your bedroom clean and comfortable and turn in for a restful night. Thank your bed.

Thank the home, its constituents and its inhabitants including you.

Connect to your clothes, shoes, accessories and of course money; to your vehicle and your 56 workplace; to your phones and computer, all things that make you successful at work. Take good care of everything and thank them.

Make a list of your favourite books, music, movies and artworks; all things that keep you happy and rooted in your cultural life. Visit these things regularly and thank them.

Sometimes we appreciate only the valuable antiques or the latest models of gadgets, but to celebrate life is to appreciate all the things that you use and need everyday.

Then connect to 'the others'. Connect to your innermost circle first and then move slowly outwards. Reaffirm the commitment in your relationships: with your partner, children, parents, siblings. Find time to appreciate them, thank them, join them in everyday life and do things together as much as you can. Do not forget to pray for them. It is important to appreciate or thank your parents for something they did for you when you were a child and it is still a happy memory to you.

Make a list of your favourite people and organize their addresses, phone numbers and e-mail IDs. If you are suddenly eager to hear your friend's voice it can be really frustrating not to have her number handy.

Make a plan; in what format and how frequently you wish to contact them. Then go about following it as much as you want to. You are a busy person and so are your friends and relatives. Don't feel bad if you can't make contacts on a regular basis. Also try to bring variations in your messages; paint or design a greeting card, send a song or a small parcel of gift or choose a nice e-card. Take particular care of those who are more likely than others to feel isolated, such as the elderly and the infirm or the disabled.

On the other hand if you don't like to plan and want to ride on spontaneity, go ahead.

Connect through prayer on a regular basis for the well-being of the family and all near and dear ones. Pray for everything that is close to your heart. Go over a list of people and things. A lengthy prayer may not be possible everyday, even a short one will do.

If you have understood and accepted the concept of such a prayer, just say, 'I do connect to everyone', that's it.

Make animals and plants your friends. Fortunate are those who like gardening or love pets. The satisfaction you get by looking after your plants is very special, particularly when you see them grow and flower. The warmth you feel when you cuddle your pets is unique. Talk to them, seek their good wishes and pray for them. Remember that it is often the plants and the animals that help us in becoming human in the true sense.

One of my friends had some indoor plants that would not do well. Some would wilt in a short while, others would remain stunted. Was the lighting insufficient, was the watering inadequate, were they undernourished, she could not understand. A lot of worrying and fussing did not help. Standardized suggestions like playing music to them did not work much either. The focus was all the time on the plants and a little irritation had started growing. There was a point when she had contemplated having no plants at all.

Then things started changing. Friends brought in new plants as gifts. Some acquaintances unexpectedly taught her better ways of handling them. My friend began to feel that her relationship with the plants was improving. Occasionally she found herself communicating with them. Talking is not the exact word, but the closest word for this kind of communication.

She felt as if once she stopped focusing too much on the problem and started taking in the wider picture, only then the benefits came.

Connect yourself with your habitat. Do something for the preservation and the betterment for your environment. It could be in any area: cleanliness and pollution control; traffic; watchfulness and security, etc.

You are a part of your society, your people. Whatever you can do to help others in your community will link you with them strongly.

Try to forge new relationships: with people, places, ideas, and activities. Develop them slowly while maintaining contacts with your existing relationships in the same areas.

Compassion is perhaps the most humane of all qualities. The ability to feel the pain of another individual is crucial. Be kind to others, particularly to the children and the elderly; the needy and the feeble; the unwell and the disadvantaged. Helping is one of the best ways of connecting   58 to people as is praying for them. Do whatever you can.

A simple method can bind you with the five 'Elements', described in the ancient texts. Through them you can feel the connections to everything and everybody else because the universe is made of those basic elements. Hold a pebble in your palm and feel connected to 'Earth'. Take a couple of deep breaths and feel the connection with 'Air'. Sip a mouthful of 'Water' and get connected to it. Light a candle and feel the connection with 'Fire'. Finally look at the sky and feel connected to 'Space'.

Last but not the least; feel connected to the ultimate and the inexhaustible source of existence, knowledge and joy: the Supreme Consciousness. Stay firm in your faith and try to be relentless in your prayer.

Connectedness is not an end-state. It is an ever-expanding process starting with you and going on to encompass the universe. What all and how much you wish to feel connected with is entirely up to you. The whole exercise of connections is voluntary, there is no compulsion. You should be at the helm of your activities of connection as with most other things in your life.

Being well-connected is being healthy. The feelings of isolation and alienation will dissipate slowly as you get more and more rooted in life. A quiet awareness of strength and contentment will eventually engulf you.

Will-Power

Will power is the real power behind our projects, big or small. Any kind of positive self-change requires a good deal of motivation. Such a change could be transitory or long-lasting. It may be achieved with ease or difficulty, depending on the amount of motivation invested in it.

For many of us the following are possibly common expressions, 'I cannot change my habits,' or even 'I think my situation will never change'. It is a daunting task to bring about any change albeit small in your behaviour.

You are a person of strong habits, good as well as bad. But you have realized that changing 'you' though difficult, may still be possible. Trying to change 'another person' is definitely much more difficult, if not nearly impossible. Even if she does change it has to occur through her motivation and not yours.

The clue lies in being modest about it. If you aim to change a small part of yourself, a small behaviour or even a miniscule part of behaviour, then it is possible.

One needs a power of will to bring about a self-change. Enhancing this will power is not easy. There have been many suggestions, from inspirational literature to behaviour therapy techniques to meditation. A simple yet practicable approach is suggested here, called the 'Deprivation Exercises'.

The idea is to deprive you of some specific privileges for a specific period of time. This privilege could be a favourite thing, a preferred activity or a faculty of the body. The degree of deprivation should be mild to moderate. It should never be severe or damaging in any way. Further, it should not harm any other person. If you have any doubts about the health-related issues such as the fasting, please consult your doctor first.

The aim is to cause a mild irritation in the mind for a brief period. You must experience the irritation, withstand it and resist the temptation to bring an end to the process of deprivation. This way you will learn to handle the process.

Slowly you will be able to increase the frequency and also the magnitude of the particular deprivation. As a result your capacity to withstand the irritation will enhance. Eventually your will power will become better.

61

Such a stronger will power could then be utilized to bring about other desirable self-changes within yourself. For example, if you can partially stay away from using your dominant hand, you would perhaps feel stronger about cutting down your smoking. You might be saying to yourself: "If I am strong enough to handle one, why not the other?"

There is one more suggestion. Start the process when you are happy. Then you can face the demand of bringing about a change which you may otherwise consider quite difficult. During your period of happiness you are both brave and generous. Not only do you feel venturesome to try out a task, you are also less stingy about spending your energy and effort towards that task. Therefore the best time to try out the methods of deprivation is when you feel reasonably happy.

Doing without 'The Things':

These are the comforts, privileges and pleasurable activities of everyday life that you may chose to live without for varying periods of time. Try living:

1. Without newspapers, magazines and TV: You should be careful about deprivation regarding these. Deprive yourself partially or only for a short while or change the timings of your information intake. Or try substituting one with another, for example, replace watching television news with reading the newspaper or vice versa. Even a short deprivation can be quite distressing for people habituated to their morning newspaper or to their evening TV serial.

2. Without the computer: This too can be difficult for game buffs or internet addicts. Moderation in the deprivation remains the answer.

3. Without foods and beverages: In a mild form of deprivation it would be missing your favourite food items from a list. Or it could be avoiding specific ingredients such as salt, sugar

62

or oil. In a more advanced form it could be fasting with different grades of severity. Fasting should preferably be for short periods, not done routinely and always easy to practice. Your health should not suffer in any way.

4. Without drinking and smoking: All intake of such substances should preferably be moderate and under control. When you decide to deprive yourself from your usual intake you should do it slowly and after some deliberation. Otherwise the irritation resulting from the deprivation may become difficult to handle and there could be a risk of an increased intake of the substance on the rebound.

If drinking and smoking are already your problem areas, do not try the deprivation involving them. Rather accept them as such and seek expert help about them.

Doing without 'The Senses':

The idea in this section is to bring in the deprivation in the use of four out of our five sense organs: sight, hearing, taste and touch. Since smelling is inseparably linked with breathing this deprivation should not be tried at all.

All these exercises should be done very carefully, always in a safe environment and for brief periods only. The idea is to experience the deprivation and not to learn how to live without a particular faculty.

1. Without Sight: Since the majority of all our sensory inputs are visual, not being able to see even for a brief period creates a strong sense of deprivation. There are various methods: switching off all lights during night ('black-out'), using heavy drapes in closed-door situations during daytime and easiest of all, getting blindfolded. You should make sure to perceive no light at all and be guided primarily by hearing and touch. Again this should be done strictly within a zone of safety.   63

You should not move all over the house without
your sight.

I have had the habit of retiring and switching the lights
off with a pen and a notepad. Then I would think up something,
a couplet or even a storyline in a few sentences. And I wrote in
the complete darkness with a steady hand judging the margins
of the page and the distance between the lines entirely by touch.
If I could check the temptation and wrote no more than a few
sparse lines on a single page, I would be safe. Otherwise, as it
frequently happened, a line would be overwritten by another
and then by yet another and I could not decipher the jumble at
all the next morning. Many earth-shattering ideas had been lost
this way!
At times I had tried making stencils cut out on a piece of
cardboard to provide the spaces for the lines. It worked somewhat better but was not entirely fool-proof.

2. Without Hearing: Cutting down the sound inputs to
   a minimum may be particularly difficult in today's
   urban world. The timing for such exercises should
   therefore be chosen when it is relatively quiet. Using cotton balls as ear-plugs may not be entirely
   satisfactory. Using headphones without the audio
   may be more useful. Now a day you may try using
   speciality headphones designed to eliminate outside
   noise. Watching the TV with the sound muted can
   be another useful method.

This deprivation too should be practised with great care
and always with the safety issues in mind.

3. Without Taste: Eating something that is diminished
   in taste is important; not merely chewing something
   tasteless such as gum. Boiled eggs or mashed pota-
   toes without salt and semolina or rice pudding without sugar would be common examples. Plain oats
   porridge is a nearly tasteless substance. Partial deprivation of taste can also be tried such
   as omitting salad dressing, mustard or   64

ketchup with food, reducing the amount of season-
ing and garnishing or using salt or sugar in reduced
quantities.

There are some cultural practices in which people keep
special fasts for a day by eating everyday food without salt or by
eating only uncooked food.

4. Without Touch: Omitting all sensations of touch is
   difficult to attain. What should be aimed for is a diminished sensation. Try handling household things
   wearing gloves made of different thickness and
   materials (e.g. latex, wool, cloth). Be careful not to
   break things. Don't try to touch hot, cold or abrasive
   surfaces.

Doing without 'The Tools'

Deprivation can be attempted in a similar, careful way
with 'the tools'. These are the upper limbs, the lower limbs and
speech. Practicing deprivation in this section is more complex
and should be attempted with additional caution and care.
Sometime you may need the help of an understanding friend.
You have to be innovative to restrict the usage of one or both
sides of your limbs, depending on how difficult you want to
make it.

1. Without Upper Limbs: Not using the upper limbs at
   all would mean doing almost nothing. You should
   try not to use different parts of the limb. Be careful
   not to drop things. Here are some examples:

   a. Try to replace your dominant upper limb with
      the non-dominant one. For example, trying to
      write with your left hand can be quite challeng-
      ing. Again the idea is to feel the deprivation and
      not to learn to write with the left hand.
   b. Put the hand in a ball-glove by putting a ball
      of cotton in the palm, curling your
      fingers around it and bandaging the   65

whole hand. Try handling and holding different objects with the gloved hands.

c. Tie both hands together and try to work keeping them tied.

d. Put one of your upper limbs in a sling or tie it behind your back.

e. Try to do with your elbows what you would normally do with your hands.

2. Without Lower Limbs: You can hobble on your toes or can waddle on your heels. Or you can fold or even tie one of your legs behind the thigh and hop around. Be careful not to fall.

3. Without speech: This could be the easiest or the most difficult exercise, depending on how co-operative your associates are. Remaining mute while one is alone doesn't count. You should be in a social situation required to speak naturally. Instead, you try to communicate either by writing or by using some sort of sign language.

Never tie any body part too tightly and for long periods to avoid the risk of impaired blood circulation.

Please don't do anything that you don't want to. Bring variations as much as you like. Stop anytime if you feel uncomfortable. Keep safe above all else.

The major gain accrued from these techniques is going to be an enhancement of your will-power. Application of that power in different walks of your life will still require careful planning.

A colleague of mine rightly suggested that these techniques could also help you get in touch with yourself. There can also be a renewal of creativity.

Relationships

Hierarchy of Relationships

You are a social person like other human beings. You and others are related to one-another in various ways. There are relatives, friends, colleagues, neighbours; the list can go on and on. You are not equally close to all of them; there are different levels of emotional closeness.

A model of relationships is suggested that may serve as a tool for appraisal as well as change. It describes different relationships keeping you as the point of reference. What you actually feel and do for the other person at each level is important. It is your approach towards her that determines your particular level of relationship with her.

There are varying levels of emotional bonding and interpersonal comfort. They are organized in the form of a hierarchy in which the higher level subsumes the characteristics of the lower ones but the reverse situation does not happen.

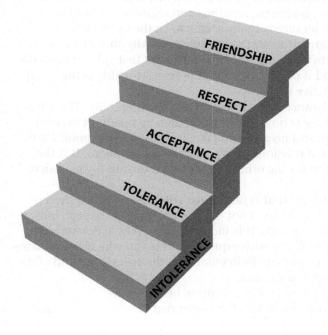

67

Try to approach this model from the lowermost level. It is called 'Tolerance'. As the name implies, here you are aware mainly of the other person's negative aspect.

What you don't like about the person dominates your mind and you become upset or even angry. But you are in control of your emotions and you have decided to tolerate her in spite of the negative side. It takes a conscious effort to tolerate someone's negative qualities.

She would also have a positive side but you choose to remain oblivious of it. Also you do not wish to belong to her or to have any truck with her. She just happens to share the same time and space in this world with you.

We might as well examine the issue of 'Intolerance' at this point. In the scope of this hierarchy, Intolerance would be something even lower than Tolerance. Indeed it is and at the level of Intolerance no meaningful relationship is possible. If you cannot even tolerate somebody why should you go for a relationship with her?

What we see around us today is largely Intolerance on various grounds and on varying pretexts. If we consider the many ethnic, linguistic, religious and regional conflicts among people, Intolerance actually seems to be the order of the day. When you are intolerant about someone why should you feel compelled to behave sensibly toward her? Instead you may like to insult and if possible hurt that person. Hostility is the usual response, active or passive.

Tolerance is the lowermost in the hierarchy. Though at this level there is no sense of belonging, no resultant expectations and almost no give and take, it is the starting point for the other levels of relationship if you wish to have them. It is the starting point for the other levels of relationship if you wish to have them.

The level that is just above Tolerance is called 'Acceptance'. Here the focus is not only on the negative aspect, but on the individual as such. It is indeed on the 'Whole Person' with negative as well as positive qualities. It is you who chooses to accept her as a complete individual with the co-existing and often conflicting characteristics.

You are in reality accepting her as an acquaintance or a member of the extended family.   68

Acceptance signifies a benevolent relationship in which the other person becomes a member of your society. An emotional bond, howsoever weak, starts getting forged at this level. But the mutual expectation may not be high and the reciprocity is usually low.

Let us examine the next level. It is called 'Respect'. Here you change your focus again and choose to preferentially consider the positive qualities in the person. You start to respect her for those qualities. You may even choose to ignore the negative side she has. There could be a lot of praise and admiration for the person, yet you may not feel very close. Usually there would be some emotional distance.

The bond that is developed at the level of Acceptance becomes stronger here. When you respect somebody you tend to expect a high standard of behaviour from her. The amount of give and take also increases.

The high level of emotional closeness that is missing at Respect comes at the next level. This is the fourth and the highest in the hierarchy and is called 'Friendship'. Here the focus changes again and you feel close enough to the individual to start noticing some of her problems.

These problems may be major or minor. They may be related to a life situation like someone's illness in the family. Or they may be a part of her personality such as quick-temperedness. In either condition you feel concerned and want to do something in your capacity to help. It could be a logistic act of helping such as baby-sitting to tide over the family's difficult situation. Or it could be a friendly suggestion to tone down her angry flare-ups. It could even be a prayer to help her out in a crisis.

It is this urge of caring that sets Friendship apart from its preceding levels. You usually drop your guard and try to belong to the friend completely. The expectations are quite high and the reciprocal behaviour is enhanced. You start feeling responsible toward the person not only for her life situations but also for her attitudes and actions. At this level you want the individual to live a happier and fuller life. And you want to be happy about her happiness.

You can think clearly of the persons with whom you are at the level of Friendship. Some have been your 'Friends' for years, others might have been recent developments.

In this hierarchy, Friendship is the highest level of relationship between you and the other person. 'Love' is not at another level, any higher than Friendship. Love is understood as a special kind of friendship that additionally involves a strong (and exclusive) mutual attraction. There is also a tendency to have proximity; you want to live close to the person you love. If you are separated geographically, you wish to keep in regular touch. In addition there is a kind of pressure, an urgency, to help or to do something worthwhile for the loved one.

There is not much difference quality-wise, between the different kinds of love; parental, filial and romantic. None is higher or lower than any other. Only the special fragrance of each love-relationship is different. Love between close friends from either the same or different genders comes very close. All types of love share the central features of high emotional closeness and inter-dependence. When you are in a love relationship, the urge of giving often surpasses that of receiving. You also experience increased preoccupation with the loved one.

It is clear that Tolerance is subsumed under Acceptance, Acceptance is included in Respect and Respect is embedded in Friendship. The lower level has to be achieved and assimilated before reaching for the higher one. They have to be attained sequentially, like climbing up the steps and none can be jumped, ideally speaking.

These levels become transitional in an evolving relationship. It is possible, at least theoretically, to mobilize many, if not most of your relationships from the level of Tolerance to that of Friendship. A reverse movement is also possible, in which a person who previously enjoyed a position of Respect in relation to you, may slip down to Acceptance or even to Tolerance.

Upwards or downwards, the movement is almost always along the sequence, usually stopping (and taking stock) at all levels. One does not usually skip Respect and climb to Friendship directly from Acceptance; nor does one slide directly from Friendship to Tolerance, bypassing the middle steps. Rarely, when the relationship improves or deteriorates very quickly, such bypassing may be seen.

In very unusual circumstances somebody may come down precipitously from Friendship to Intolerance, skipping the steps altogether, as if by jumping off the precipice from the other side. This may only occur when there is a sudden breach of basic trust giving rise to sudden and major hostility.

At each level, not only you but the other person is also participating in the relationship. The involvement is hardly ever fifty-fifty but it has to be substantial from either side to make the relationship work. Over a period of time, the same individual may slide up or down the levels depending on the situations and the resultant changes in the attitudes from both sides.

An example would perhaps make it clearer. Suppose you met this woman in your neighbourhood who has recently moved in and has a reputation of being discourteous and even rude. Initially you felt repulsion as you could not stand rudeness; later decided to just tolerate, but not to have anything to do with her.

Then one day you saw her playing and singing with the neighbourhood children. You felt surprised and happy because you too like kids. That changed your stand towards her and you started accepting her as a neighbour. You talked to each-other at a party and felt comfortable about it.

Later you learned that she was an accomplished singer. Music too had always been one of your loves, so you began respecting her musical expertise and talent. Gradually you both started meeting periodically and discuss and share music.

Still later the closeness between you increased and you started sharing personal stories with each-other. You were always concerned with her lapses of rude behaviour. One day you felt particularly confident and brought the topic up. She too did not perceive this as an intrusion and in fact agreed that it was one of her problems. When you both discussed it at length, it became clear that her rude behaviour was probably a façade to hide her deep-rooted lack of self-esteem. It was surprising, given her worldly musical accomplishments.

You offered to go along with her to a counsellor, if she so wished. She finally agreed to go, alone. Eventually she underwent counselling to tackle her self-esteem issues. In this whole process she became your friend. A great system of care gradually developed between the two of you.

This model is best understood when you consider your relationship with a single person. It also works when you are trying to relate to a group of people as a reasonably homogeneous entity. It is applicable to the relationships happening across any age range.

An example concerning a group could be that of a new teacher trying to form a relationship with a class of students who already exist as a close-knit group. She may learn to just tolerate the noisy unruly behaviour and keep herself aloof as a person. Or she may progress to accepting them with a curious mixture of bad and good behaviour or she may even start respecting them for their remarkable academic work. It will, however, remain a daunting task if she were to be actively involved in the all-round growth of the students and try to better their training through caring support. That would really be a journey toward Friendship with the class.

An act of volition is central to the process of building a relationship. What you want to do is of primary importance. Going back to the example of the person whom you could barely tolerate (at the beginning of the relationship), you were really saying to yourself: 'I can just about tolerate this person. I do not aspire to accept her because I don't want to.' Your stand at that point was crucial. Had you really then and there wanted to accept her as a fellow being, perhaps you could? But you chose to remain upset about her rude outbursts and stopped at the level of Tolerance.

If you had chosen to remain at that Tolerance level regarding her, that would have been a valid choice as well. Even though it is ideal and possible, at least theoretically, to be at the level of Acceptance with everyone; in real life Tolerance is the level where many people would stay. It may not be possible to accept everybody.

What you want to do with a relationship is therefore largely in your hands. It would be a good idea to make a list of your major existing relationships. Try to match where each person fits on your hierarchy. This will give you a clearer picture of your own position vis-à-vis these important individuals in your life. Your own appraisal is the only way to place a particular person at a particular level. This hierarchy should work equally well with relatives and friends. Past relationships may also be appraised as an exercise in hindsight.

These considerations about relationships have a direct bearing on how you view the institutions of family and community. When you were a child there was a lot of positive input from your parents, caregivers, elders. Even if that was not true in your case, it should have been ideally. There is a saying that 'it takes a whole village to raise a child'. It means each caring person contributes, at least a little and brings her own special qualities to benefit the young person.

All those elders possibly considered you at the level of Friendship. They were patient with you as you handled your moods; anger, joy, sorrow and excitement. They were supportive to you as an inquisitive youngster. As you grew up you continued to have them at the level of Friendship. Children usually are quite caring about their care-giving adults.

In the world outside home it was a different picture. All through your school years you had numerous people at different degrees of intimacy. The 'bully' was understandably at the level of Tolerance; most of the classmates were at Acceptance and a few of them were at Respect.

Those few, who had reached the level of Friendship with you in your school days and later as adults and have not moved below the level of Respect, are precious for you. Nurture this handful of relationships. These are the few people with whom Tolerance and Acceptance come naturally and usually in abundance.

As you grow into a fine young person, sometimes there are mounting pressures for new relationships. Be careful about how you proceed. Before you become emotionally very close, please take care that the other person is definitely at the level of Friendship with you, if not at the level of Love. In this way if the relationship clicks and proceeds towards a long-term partnership or marriage, you will have an advantage because the other person is already at a high level of resonance. If it does not click unfortunately, you will still be on safe grounds because of the same reason. You will continue to remain on the level of at least Respect, if not at Friendship itself.

Avoid haste even when you become comfortable in the love relationship. Do not plan babies unless you are reasonably sure that your partnership is going to continue for a long period.   73

Do try to relate to your children from the level of Acceptance upwards if not from Respect. If they are at Friendship or Love, such a relationship is most beneficial for children. It is going to nurture them and make your life easy as a parent.

Do also try to build a social network based on Friendship or Respect in which you can participate along with your partner and children as a family unit.

Try to save the marriage or the partnership as far as possible. While it lasts, it saves many lives emotionally, least of all those of the children. If you have difficulty sorting things out by yourselves, it is useful to seek the counsel of the well-wishers or professional help.

Go for a clean-cut break-up, if the love relationship can not be saved in spite of the best efforts of the partners. Try to be fair and non-damaging as much as possible, thereby remaining at the level of Respect with each-other, if not at Friendship.

Do try to remain at Friendship with your children if not at Love. Take care not to let them be mistreated in any way. Rather if you happen to suspect neglect or abuse in any situation, please report and take measures.

This hierarchical model of relationship provides you with the essentials. It is then up to you to decide whether you want a person to remain at the existing level of emotional closeness or you want her to move up or down. If you choose the latter option it is going to be another exercise.

To move anybody up the hierarchy you will need to do a lot of positive emotional work primarily with yourself and then with the concerned individual. This means taking overall better care of you and then working tirelessly and reaching out. The other person's reactions to your actions will doubtless remain important. But the result will depend primarily on your volition and motivation.

There are many positive things that we possess naturally as children. We lose those qualities slowly as we grow up. Being able to relate spontaneously to others comes easily to children. How can we preserve those qualities at least partially? I agree that the demands of an adult life are difficult. But it is perhaps not right to forget how comfortably you used to become close to others, including the elders. Relearning about it and regaining any part of it will be important. 74

Living with the family

Hyper focusing/Defocusing/Refocusing:

People live alone or with others once they reach adult-hood. Prior to that, many if not most, live with others; often with the members of the family. An adult may choose to live alone, start living-together or continue to live with their parents and siblings.

Living with others can be a nice, as well as a difficult thing. On one hand you receive a lot of support and nurturance. On the other you also get a lot of unwarranted attention, inter-ference and possibly hostility. It is the latter situation that I am talking about.

If there is someone as an identified 'Unwell Person'; of-ten the rest of the family assumes a peculiar position. It appears as if only the unwell person has any problems whatsoever and everybody else is perfectly all right. As a result, the other mem-bers concentrate on the unwell person's life much to the exclu-sion of their own. Thus a kind of vicarious living starts in which the 'Well' members become engrossed in the unwell member's life and their problems. They have little to talk about anything else.

This situation is called 'Hyper focused'. Often such talk continues throughout the day with many critical and even hostile comments. Such emotion-laden comments have been described as 'Expressed emotions' in mental health parlance and they are known to worsen some of the existing mental disorders (Leff and Vaughn 1981).

The individual who is unwell mostly suffers in silence. When she can not endure it any more, she starts retaliating ver-bally. This often leads to bitter quarrels. In some rare cases there can also be physical violence. In any case the communication be-comes poor and the relationships deteriorate. Such a condition not only spells a poor prognosis for the affected person but also hinders the well-being of the other members of the family.

There is another point. Quarrelling and heated exchang-es generate a lot of negative emotions, mainly anger, but also anxiety and depression. Once they happen they kind of fulfil some of our craving for emotions in 75 everyday life. For a person whose life doesn't have many positive emotions, any emotional exchange, even the negative ones become welcome. As a result many of us like a good quarrel. We often feel strangely alive, once a round of intense negative exchanges has taken place. This is one of the reasons why fights tend to perpetuate in families.

There is a way out of this impasse. It is a kind of contract that the family has to agree to and engage in. I would encourage you as one of the non-affected members to start to concentrate on your own individual life. Starting to solve some long-standing problems or to develop some new hobbies could be beneficial. In order to do this you will have to bring down your level of over-involvement with the affected member. I call these 'Refocusing' and 'Defocusing' respectively.

There is a method which facilitates this process. First of all the family should be ready to identify and acknowledge the problem of Hyper focusing. Then they should agree to address the problem. They must realize that there are vicious cycles which need to be broken. Hyper focusing often leads to an accentuation of negative behaviour in the person who is unwell, resulting in further Hyper focusing.

Positive as well as neutral comments could be given at any time. But there should be no negative comments throughout the day except for a specifically designated circumscribed period. Such a specific time slot may be called a 'Discussion Forum'. The exact timing and duration should be mutually agreed upon. Negative comments (critical/hostile/over-involved) should be restricted only to that period.

Once the negative things are spoken they give rise to some heated discussion. It is quite common to lose one's temper if the discussion turns nasty. Therefore all members should ensure that nobody becomes angry beyond a point. If someone does become very angry it will be her responsibility to control the runaway emotions.

To facilitate it, the angry individual (again you, as an example) would need to leave the meeting physically, move away and try to control the anger using distraction methods, etc. If the anger does come down quickly, you may come back and rejoin the discussion. If it does not, then you will have to wait for the slot of the next 'Discussion Forum',   76

which may be the
next day. Thus some issues will be carried over from one day to
another and will be resolved only slowly.

All emotionally charged exchanges, even the negative
ones, are habit-forming. It is difficult to get rid of them. This
exercise should continue day after day, until the family reaches
a lowered level of negative interactions. If it happens eventually,
everybody benefits, not only the unwell individual. But practicing these remedial methods is difficult even if understanding the
underlying theory is not.

If you are the person who is unwell in such a family you
will have to work hard to achieve the new system of focusing in
the family. If you are one of them who perpetuate the Hyper-
focusing you will have to work harder.

One of the young women I saw a few years back came
from a dysfunctional family. She was the only child and very
sensitive from early childhood. The parents were over-involved
and quite controlling. They were fairly successful people otherwise.

Around late adolescence the client started having some
differences with the parents. While this would be common in
many families, in this particular family the situation became
rough quickly. The parents overcame their own differences and
united to discipline her. The arguments gave way to shouting
matches, calling names and even to physical violence. When I
saw them the client was an inpatient and the parents were stay-
ing with her.

I started seeing the client in individual therapy involving
other modules of 'Luminous Life'. After a few sessions I realised
that Hyper focusing was continuing in their family. It was made
worse by the parents' renewed hostile remarks, as they found it
difficult to cope with their daughter trying to change for the better.

Then I invited the parents for a few family sessions and
worked with them using the techniques of this module: Hyper-,
De- and Refocusing. Initially there was a lot of resistance from
the parents. As would be expected, they thought that all problems were only the daughter's and not theirs. They continued to
protect themselves as well as to blame her. Only after much deliberation could they see the benefits of   77

this approach. Gradually the client as well as her parents became familiar with Defocusing and Refocusing and the vicious cycle was ultimately broken.

When the client finished individual therapy I called the whole family again for a session of summing-up. Everybody expressed their satisfaction with the new situation. I was recently in touch with them after a gap of years and it was heartening to see that they all were still in a harmonious relationship.

Sometimes the psychological problems of the family are very deeply rooted and the approaches mentioned above are not enough to help them. They would perhaps need formal and more substantial family therapy. Nonetheless these methods could be given a fair trial in many dysfunctional families before considering further expert professional inputs.

Additional Modules

Time

Your life is limited on two sides by birth and death. In between there is a span of years that is life. This may be seen as a collection of a few decades or as millions of seconds depending on what you are trying to communicate. The fact remains that it is a finite period.

Death is a reality that many if not most of us remain oblivious of. Why this is so cannot be answered easily; not briefly anyway. But this phenomenon has been known for a long time. The Mahabharata has a famous story about it where Yudhisthira speaks to the Yaksa:

> *"Ahanyahani bhūtāni, gacchantīha yamālayam*
> *Śesāh sthāvaramicchanti kimāścaryamatah param"*

> *'When asked 'what is the wonder of the world'; Yudhisthira answered, 'Creatures die everyday. Even after seeing this people think that they are going to live forever. What other wonder can compare to this?'*

> *(Mahabharata/Vanaparva/313/116; Manjul-Manjusha: 173)*

This life is all that you have got. This is perhaps your only resource, the only currency that you can spend. And we know that this is true for every other living being in this universe. Therefore it is very important for you to handle time carefully. This is ultimately your life.

Time is something that you spend each moment; for yourself, for others, with work, with leisure, in agony and in ecstasy. When committing to anything you are essentially committing your time to that thing.

It is really up to you how organized or otherwise you are in managing your time. Consult a good source for time management. Learn the basic techniques and stick to them. They are deceptively easy to understand and decidedly tough to implement. As with most things you will require   79 a good deal of motivation to put into practice the techniques of managing your time better. But it is worth trying every time.

Examining your past commitments might be a useful way to re-prioritize your future ones. Think about your elders; parents in particular. If your relationship with them had been harmonious ask yourself if the quantity as well as the quality of the time you had spent with them in the recent years was all right or otherwise. If you think you have not spent enough good times with them then perhaps you would like to start doing it to the extent your life permits it. Elders are a priority because they will be the first ones to leave you in the usual scheme of things. So re-channel your attention to them and correct the major gaps if any.

Maybe it will need visiting or spending quality time with them more often, maybe trying to help them more with their needs or maybe even just calling them to say you love them, miss them, wanted to thank them, anything really. Whatever you decide, practice it and stick to your new pattern.

Review it after a gap, say a few months. You will be surprised to see how fulfilling to you this 'Re-allocation of Time' exercise has been. If you love your elders you will never regret deciding to spend more of your most valuable resource – your time – with them.

You may choose to do the same exercise with your children if they are still growing up. Try the same with your partner, your close friends, siblings, and other near and dear ones. The results are likely to be strikingly similar.

This happens because you are essentially acknowledging the unstoppable flow of time, actually realizing that everybody is becoming older by the day if not by the hour. You are also trying to do something positive about it.

You are in fact attempting to spend more of your time with, for and about the people whom you love, who are important to you. In essence you are targeting what is included in the 'Important' section of the time management book, only trying to do things in a 'Non-Urgent' manner.

Negotiation

When you were a small child perhaps your world used to revolve around you in a different sense than it does now. Then your wishes were supreme and your views were sacrosanct. Your authority was unquestionable to you. As a baby you remained in a world where you could afford not to consider the other person's point of view.

But that world changed fairly quickly as you started growing up. Then you had to learn to respect the wishes of others apart from those of your own. This perhaps was one of biggest challenges of becoming an adult. You should be happy that you have learned to do that.

Negotiation is the hallmark of a mature adult human interaction. In negotiation you retain some of your ground while leaving some of it depending on the need of the situation. You listen to your demands as well as to those of the other person. In this process you respect yourself and the person you are dealing with.

Negotiation therefore is to be your mode of interaction with the world, not coercion or manipulation. You want to get your fair share in the deal and you do not want to exploit others if you can help it. You should want to do this everyday, at home, in the workplace, everywhere.

You give some to get some. The spirit of the negotiating process can be expressed in one pair of words: 'Sharing and Fairness'. Take care that you are unfair neither to you nor to the other party.

Consider the common example of a drinks party. The canapé are being served. You are there with a few others. When the tray comes near what do you do? Many of us choose the better-looking pieces habitually. A minority of us take the not-so-good ones, again habitually. It is suggested that you try to change your usual pattern and see how you feel. Whether your strong point is doing that extra-bit for yourself or for others it will be an important exercise. Chances are you will not feel too bad either way.

Think about watching TV shows, a common enough occurrence. You have all gathered in the living room after a hard day's work. You wish to watch a serial,   81 your partner a sports program, your child a cartoon. Everybody wants to watch her or his program on the large screen. Instead of making others watch your favourite show or worse still having to watch the program the others like, you can start a negotiating process.

To begin with all slots are to be short and definitely not too long. Preferably the needs of all members should be listed and then prioritised depending on the situation. Children's time in front of a lighted screen should ideally be rationed, plus they often have the requirement of going to bed earlier than the grown-ups. So sometimes the child finishes the short stint and goes off thanking you.

Next, either you or the partner has it depending on how important the situation is, such as a championship match or an important debate. The non-watching person may read a book, enjoy something else or do a chore. After the particular show the situation is reversed. If you both like the same or at least similar programs then the field should be all yours once the young one is gone!

This is just a suggestion. You are sure to come up with your own creative solutions every time there is a situation demanding the adult negotiating approach.

Negotiation is not about bending others and making them do something you like, but it is about re-adjusting everybody's needs including yours. You can not negotiate until and unless you are there as an active participant.

Creativity

Being creative is one of the characteristics of human beings that along with superior intelligence have been responsible for most of the achievements so far. Someone can be creative in a general sense or more commonly it can be a specific attribute. Creativity can be quite useful and that is the focus here.

Do not ask yourself: Am I creative? Of course you are. In fact everybody is. It is similar to intelligence in a way. The quantity, quality and in particular the variety of creative force is different in different individuals. The question to ask is: In what quarters am I most creative? Depending on the answers you get, start building a niche for yourself.

When you are being creative it is essentially happening within you. You are becoming creative for yourself. You are asserting the multi-dimensionality that is essentially human. Doing things by yourself with limited use of machines gives you an advantage. Little craftwork, like making greetings cards or writing letters or singing bring out your unique characteristics.

Start doing whatever you are good at, whatever you like doing best. Creative activities need not be prescriptive or stereotyped. Everybody doesn't need to paint murals or to write short stories. Do what appeals to your heart.

You will find that even a little bit of creative input makes life more interesting. It is essential to bring in your own touch in what you do. It should be either solely your creation as in a poem or your creative twist in something commonplace, say in dressing up. Your business suit may be like everybody else's but the accessories may bear a mark of your specific choice. From briefcases to handbags, there are various alternatives so that your individual choice is better exercised.

Start anywhere: cooking, organizing the living room, telling stories to children, arranging birthday parties. In the family life you don't have to be the creative lead if you don't want to. If your partner or the child can do it better, let them. You just join the team and have fun. The creative endeavours of one member can very well be complementary to those of the others. Perhaps the ethos of creativity is important rather than the activities themselves.

83

Creativity breaks monotony, and rekindles interest in life. The emphasis should not be on: 'every time something innovative has to be done'. It should be a spontaneous process, enjoyable as well as useful. You and your dear ones are the best judge: when and how to be creative about something and also how much.

Human beings have produced a bewildering array of highly creative pursuits, over the centuries, across the cultures. Why not be aware of them and appreciate them as much as they are accessible? Being able to enjoy creative art, music or writing is one of the blessings of life. Also appreciating the creative works serves as an inspiration and sometimes as a catalyst for your own creativity.

I knew a man closely. He had been creative all through his simple life. The limited means could never curb his genius. He was a great story-teller and you could imagine his popularity as a teacher of history. Apart from rooftop gardening where he used the most unlikely earthenware as pots, he wrote devotional songs, composed the music and sang them. He was a lover of world literature and wrote personal journals rich in philosophy. His handwriting was fine in three languages and he was fond of writing letters. No work was too big or small for him. He would smile and do something nice about a multitude of everyday things. He led a life rich in love and kindness. His creativity was an extension of him.

Celebrate the 'Common Person'

There are various methods of remaining well, of keeping yourself content. You have learned something about generating happiness in everyday activities.

Learning to value others is important. As you grew up as an adult there were many people who had supported and enriched you. Focus on all the positive inputs you have received from them, admire their worth and thank them for all their help, wherever possible. Try to recall each kind word or gesture, each good deed, every bit of help in real life.

Think of your parents, other elders and teachers. Consider your siblings, cousins and friends. It is not that those people did not have their limitations, but so do all of us. It is your choice to focus either on the limitations of people or on their generosity. What do you wish to remember: the things you did not get or the bounties you received?

Perhaps they had worked hard to raise you, faced difficulties to support you and tried utmost to train you. Perhaps they could not do many things that needed doing. But they were all human beings with many kinds of material, emotional and attitudinal limitations. They had their own follies.

They might not have been great achievers. They were definitely not the celebrities. But they were the providers, protectors, problem solvers and personal teachers to

you and to themselves. They were your rescuers at difficult times. That makes them heroes for you, doesn't it?

They also were common people. They tried to live honest, hard-working and law-abiding lives. Many of them were friendly and approachable. That should make them heroes all right, if not to the world, at least to you. And of course to people like you who too were benefited by them.

Learning to celebrate the common person is important. You are one of them: unique and valuable. So were your benefactors, those friends of yours. You need to value them and communicate your positive feelings to them. They don't need this acknowledgement, you do. You need to tell them that they are your heroes.

Far-off celebrities may dazzle you with their brilliance, they may even command a lot of your respect. But how sensible is it to make them your major preoccupation? What will you achieve by finding out the minute details of their lives? How relevant to you are the statements of their life-style? Is your life similar to theirs? Do you have as much extravagance or as many indulgences? Do you need to have them?

You need to connect yourself with the right people in the right way. Try to be a participant in the celebration of the unique positive aspects of a common person. By celebrating a good person you actually move closer to celebrating yourself.

Final Major Module

Orientation For a
Possible Future Culture and Civilization

This is a projected orientation towards the future. For the present time it remains a vision, more like a dream. As opposed to the existing and continuing global human culture a different kind of culture is possible. If anything this proposed culture will evolve through the evolution of each and every participating individual. Such a change will come only gradually, possibly over a long period of time.

Consider the existing human society the culmination of a long and uninterrupted stream of conflicts and sorrows. In different forms and contexts there has been a continued emphasis on greed, exploitation and indifference. Since the beginning of recorded history we have seen endless battles and conquests. When there were periods of relative calm and stability the internal condition of any region was still regulated by deceit and intimidation. In the past few centuries this situation has been accentuated as well as globalized.

Of course such a proposition is over-simplified. The indomitable spirit of the human being has been creating a lot of positive things in spite of this continued negative culture. Human beings have always attempted to help one-another through difficult times. They have held onto their faith, have not given up hope and have strived on. A plethora of humane values have been developed and sustained even through different dark ages. They can be seen embedded in both folk and classical cultures of many countries. The commandments of all major religions and the foundations of all humane philosophies are the products of this positive process.

Consider the existing culture as the ground floor of a building that is inhabited. The proposed culture of the future can be likened to the unfinished second story of the same building. This story has not been built yet, the floor is rough and there are only a few pillars jutting up that will later link with one-another to form the walls. Eventually a roof will be laid to complete the structure. Final positioning of the doors and the

87

windows and other structures would make the space habitable.

Consider the following 'pillars' for the proposed future culture. They are largely the products of modern day thought though their origins have been in the past. These 'pillars' are indeed the philosophical advancements and are essential for building the future culture. At present only some of these philosophies are in popular practice on a large scale. We don't know as yet when and how they will all come together.

But also consider that right now they can be practicable at the level of the individual and her circle of family and friends (The microcosm). When such practices become widespread some day they will start influencing larger communities and possibly even nations (The macrocosm).

> 1. **Eco-activism:** Since time immemorial, human beings have been dependent on Nature. Until a few hundred years back, they have been living in reasonable harmony with one-another. From the time that modern science and technology started developing in an uncontrolled way the harmony has largely been destroyed. This destruction has been particularly pronounced in the last two centuries resulting in rising pollution levels, decreasing essential resources like water, different species becoming endangered (and even extinct) and threatening situations like Global Warming. Fortunately in the past few decades many people have realized that at the current rate of exploitation of Nature, life on earth can not be sustained for long. From once being an associate of Nature we have become its adversary.

As a result eco-awareness and activism has come up strongly as a social movement. Indeed, we should appreciate that our predecessors had largely preserved the earth and we should do the same for our successors. Eco-activism will definitely be one of the 'pillars' of the future civilization.

There are a number of things to do: use water, gas and electricity sensibly; use more public transport; avoid using plastic bags; segregate and dispose household waste; recycle things as much as possible; develop gardens   88 around the living areas and last but not the least, join eco-movements in your area.

2. Feminism: So far most civilizations have frankly been patriarchal, or at least largely dominated by males. Most cultures have assigned a secondary and subservient role to woman. Even today in many cultures women are denied their basic rights and opportunities. Child marriages are still practised and so is female infanticide.

Feminism, in its true essence, does not assign a dominant and exploiting role to females. Rather as a philosophy it emphasises the equality of the genders and their complementarities towards each-other. In the last couple of centuries this philosophy has had a liberating influence on human culture. It is being practiced fairly well in many segments of society. Also in many countries various social, occupational and cultural changes related to gender equality have been set in motion.

You could be aware of the potential gender-related inequalities and exploitations in everyday situations of yours. You can practice feminism by being conscious of your own preconceptions of the gender roles and by replacing them with more equal ones. Your relationships would of course mirror your convictions. There can be several examples: be willing to participate reasonably equally in all household activities such as cooking, cleaning and washing; be willing to share the outside responsibilities fairly equitably, such as driving and paying the bills; be willing to rear the children with reasonably equal participation; be open, honest and non-exploitative in your commitments, etc.

3. Controlled Materialism and Consumerism: In the modern world there is an excessive emphasis on acquiring newer and costlier things, on living the 'good life' and on enhancing the personal as well as the collective greed. Greed appears to be the dominant theme of today's global culture.

In the proposed future culture this issue needs to be dealt with strongly and directly. We shall be required to budget and limit our everyday needs. This need not be a stance of 'denunciation' but rather one of 'control and contentment'. The modern world has grown far too extended and complicated to allow a complete reversal of lifestyle. One needs to strike a balance between 'being extravagant' and 'being frugal'. This stance itself is going to be a difficult one, unless the individual makes a mind shift about becoming less consumerist.

The need for material excesses and extras should be understood as a deeply ingrained maladaptive need for the modern human being. It has been learned over the past many centuries. It can't be unlearned in a day.

What can be done is to make a shift from a largely materialistic mode of life to at least a partially non-materialistic mode. One needs to find more satisfaction from books, music, arts and sports than what has hitherto been. When such a shift gets well-established, the individual can move slowly away from those excessive attachments that relate mainly to clothes and shoes, food and beverages, house and vehicle, etc.

It is very difficult to control greed fully. Such an aspiration may be suitable for an ascetic but not for a modern citizen. What is more feasible is a kind of control over the overall greed and a kind of shift from a wholly material to a partly non-material greed.

For example you may make a conscious and deliberate effort to tone down the strong consumerist inclination. You may feel satisfied with a comfortable habitat and a nice car; they need not necessarily be the grand ones. You may also feel content with a judicious mix of fine clothing and accessories along with everyday wear. You may apply the same principle to the consumption of food and beverages. Another method of controlling one's tendency to overspend may be through the sharing of various resources with the close friends and family members.

4. Controlled growth of Science and Technology: Since the days of the European Renaissance and the Industrial Revolution, there have been tremendous developments in modern science and technology. From

the first steam engine to the interplanetary space-
ship, from the first typewriter to the internet, from
the first stethoscope to the gamma-knife, in almost
all fields of science; it has been an extraordinary
growth in building more powerful as well as more
sophisticated machines. Interestingly, all this has
happened during a relatively short span of human
civilization, particularly so in the last hundred years.
The growth curve has just shot upwards at an un-
precedented rate.

Unfortunately such a growth has not been very balanced.
The major motive behind this exceptional growth of technology
has been that of gaining economic advantage. In comparison,
the historical continuity has been ignored and the human angle
neglected.

For example in today's modern medicine there is an
overemphasis on sophisticated as well as costly investigations
and interventions. Alongside, there is an under emphasis on
linking up the expanding medical knowledge base with the existing knowledge stores of the various indigenous medicines.

Another example would be the almost vertical growth
pattern in the development of intricate electronic gadgets. A particular technology is at the risk of being outdated even before it
is marketed. Yet another example would be the building of dams
and other huge structures without careful planning, which can
potentially alter the delicate balance of Nature. Also consider the
rapid and extensive processes of urbanization where more trees
are felled, more concrete structures are built and more vehicles
are introduced on the roads every month.

Another major concern is the escalating growth of high-
technology machines of war. Within a span of a century we have
suffered from two devastating world wars and countless other
wars. We have been and are still playing with very dangerous
toys.

All this shows that the present trend of the development
of modern science and technology is neither balanced nor
harmonious. In other words, there should be better control over
their growth. Sadly that is lacking in today's world.

The future scenario would therefore need to balance the urgent preoccupations of the technological communities with the urgent needs of the general public. The greatest good for the largest number of people should be one of the major if not the most major motive.

As an individual you may not be in a position to influence this area very much, but you can definitely be a supporter, a votary, even an activist towards achieving the 'Controlled Growth of Technology'.

5. Philosophy: Everybody needs a frame of reference to deal with value-related questions. Values influence the personal as well as the impersonal aspects of life. This need has been there since ancient time and it is more relevant today than ever before.

Such a frame of reference is provided by the philosophical network that supports the existing culture. Losing touch with this network often makes one feel demoralised and anxious. All major organised religions have attempted to provide such networks in the form of Commandments. Also there are several non-religious sources of positive and pro-human philosophy. Irrespective of one's religious adherence one benefits from the guidance of the philosophy.

You can start with a set of core positive values that are important to you. Over a span of time and through various influences, your own unique philosophical system would emerge. In the future scheme of civilization many if not most people shall aspire to become practicing philosophers.

6. Spirituality: If you are a non-believer I respect your choice. This aspect of the future culture will not be of interest to you.

The core of all religions is spirituality yet it is free from the practices of any organized religion. It is about the belief in all-pervading supreme agency that guides human destiny towards positive values and meaningful living. This has been variously depicted as 'The Essence', 'The Consciousness', 'The Causation of Everything' etc.

No two person's spiritual quests are exactly the same, yet there are some identifiable common features about spirituality. The life-force is the most natural and spontaneous thing that works through all of us. We are not consciously aware of its existence most of the time. In a similar way if you have a quest and the Supreme Consciousness agrees to it, then It finds a way to bring to you what you seek. It is individualised, tailor-made and most appropriate for a particular person. Like two people going to the same place of worship, at the same time, they will have different internal journeys. This fact gives rise to different themes.

One theme is of a close, intimate, personal relationship with the Supreme Consciousness. A linked theme is that of a personalised prayer and a continuous flow of communication between the two ends. Another theme is 'Silent Knowledge' that comes directly. An aspect of spiritual growth in the person is a desire to change for the better. One becomes cleansed and purified, honest, humble and compassionate as one progresses on the path.

The future world is likely to be a place where many if not most people will be committed to spirituality in some form or another. Such a commitment is likely to help the people realize their positive potentials.

If you are a believer, please go along your own path. If you are not sure what to do, ask for help. God's help is on-line, ever present. Praying is at once the simplest and the most profound of all activities. Feel free to make your prayer as personalised as possible because it is meant to be just that. Bring in the local and the global needs, the short-term and the long-term aspirations, the personal and the impersonal requirements as and when you wish. One can pray literally for anything and everything.

7. Social networks and Voluntarism: Over the years the structure of the society has been changing in different situations and contexts. Various factors are responsible for today's urban society where an adult individual is often lonely and isolated from others.

People do form relationships and many of them continue for long periods, but the prevalence of discord is quite high. There are many broken families and many reconstituted ones. The issues of emotional and other kinds of neglect and abuse are often significant. Children are particularly badly affected by them.

The old family structure is usually not there, the previously supporting neighbourhood is hardly present and though there are many acquaintances one really has few close friends. Sharing, supporting, belonging, and nurturing: all these activities have become largely redundant. There is an over emphasis on independent living rather than on an inter-dependent one.

The proposed culture of future should try to build a society that has a better and closer network of people who are caring and supportive towards one-another. They should provide themselves emotional safety and nurturance among other things.

Commitment is an integral part of all social work. Whenever you feel committed to an issue an element of voluntarism is generated. The spirit of voluntarism is in trying to give back something useful to society. It should become one of the major driving forces in the future culture.

You can start participating in any voluntary work; there is always somebody who needs help. You also meet like-minded people in various social groups. Joining hobby-groups may not be much of a social activity, but it does provide a platform for the sharing of interests and may pave the way for further networking.

8. **Multiculturalism:** Human life is essentially multi-level, multi-dimensional and multi-faceted. The human cultural scene is understandably multi-cultural. Multiculturalism at one level is an acknowledgement of the plurality of life itself. It is amazing to note in how diverse and difficult conditions human culture can thrive. At another level, it is a bewildering experience to witness the marvel of a million people celebrating life in a billion different ways.

There are so many ethnic and linguist groups, so many celebratory practices and so much variation in living, working, eating and worshipping habits that when anyone reflects on them there is a new found sense of humility. There is so much to appreciate everywhere, so much to learn from everybody!

Unfortunately this very thing is not happening in today's world. There is a growing tendency to embrace a stereotypical world culture. It encourages and even entices people to dress, walk, speak, eat, drink, work, enjoy leisure and perhaps even think and feel in certain particular ways. It curbs individuality, discourages diversity and attempts to diminish the essential multi-dimensionality of human beings.

The future world would do well to accept multicultural-ism as a way of modern life. It should encourage a person to learn from many diverse cultures and to retain the local flavours while joining the one-world culture. Of particular importance are the indigenous native cultures, because they are still rela-tively non-industrialized and have therefore retained their own unique relationship with Nature.

You can start practicing multiculturalism by becom-ing aware and responsive to the numerous cultural ingredients around you. This would lead to your own preferences and would help you come up with your unique cultural formulation. Sur-round yourself with your favourite books, music, art, etc. and enjoy them on a regular basis. Your list of favourites should ide-ally be drawn from many different cultures.

It is vital to realize that human culture is a multi-hued, multi-textured and multi-functional fabric that metaphorically covers and in reality comforts us.

These proposed 'Pillars' of the future culture are real possibilities in the lives of individuals like you and in your im-mediate social groups. Adhere to them as much as you want and can without upsetting your life. The pillars support one-another and together they build the humane culture. But they can not find their true expressions at a larger social level at present. They can be a reality in the microcosm but not yet in the macro-cosm.

We have to try and we shall have to wait. There is an opportune time for everything. Perhaps the time of the fully-developed positive future culture is still a few centu- 95 ries away; perhaps it is just a few decades.

Summing Up

Humanistic psychology is not new and is a direct as well as logical development of the humane culture. Luminous Life is a new model of humanistic psychotherapy that grew out of my life and my work. I have presented it in the current format so as to be accessible and usable as a self-help resource.

We are coming to the end of this book now. All major and additional modules have been covered. We have gone through the theory and the suggested practices.

It must have been made clear that we are talking about a change in the way we see and relate to life; that it is an active process and that things can possibly change through deliberate and systematic efforts.

It is not necessary to work on the modules all at once. Pick up those that appeal most to you, or start with the easiest. Dwell upon the ideas, discover the links amongst them, see their relevance for you and build up the practices slowly. You are the user and the judge: find out which methods work for you, which don't.

The main idea is to work with yourself and to have a network of close family members and friends who can act as a support or simply like a sounding board when you need them. Good people are indispensable in our lives. They are the single most important component for our happiness and well-being other than our own selves.

By 'Good' I mean honest and committed people. They must be integrated in their own lives, positive-thinking and forward-looking in their view-points. It is not necessary that they be absolutely healthy or even high-functioning. It is enough that they are also in the same boat as you, handling their own problems, fighting their own battles, bettering their own lives.

Feel free to share the material with your dear ones; discuss it with them. If they agree, collaborate and practice the therapy together.

It is important to spend some quality time with your own self on a regular basis if not everyday. It may be as simple as exercising for a while, relaxing with music or even brushing your hair well. Or it may be writing a few lines in your diary or in your work file. It may be some   97 moments of quiescence during which you reflect on your thoughts or say your prayers.

If you consider yourself progressing well, think about this: life's journey is like climbing a hill path as opposed to walking a straight road. Think of a track that goes round the hill as it ascends. As you proceed you cross the distances longitudinally as well as vertically and the direction of your progress changes every time. Once you reach a landing, a place for a breather, your vistas change from what they had been at the start of your journey. You climb further and they change again. You get the best panoramic views once you reach the summit. It is the same with life. No two halts are the same, the perspectives are forever changing and as you advance in years your understanding broadens and deepens. In either example your horizons expand and enrich you.

The ancient Indian texts have talked about the three major manifestations or the three virtues of the Supreme Being, namely 'Satyam (Truth)', 'Shivam (Welfare)' and 'Sundaram (Beauty)'. It is also said that the three are in essence one.

'Agraha' means 'Striving for', as in 'Satyagraha' or 'Striving for Truth'. Similarly 'Shivagraha' will be 'Striving for Welfare' and 'Sundaragraha' will be 'Striving for Beauty'.

Mahatma Gandhi's 'Satyagraha' and 'Ahimsa (Non-Violence)' are perhaps the two most profound humane innovations in the history of humankind (Fischer 1982). These humanistic concepts as the solutions for interpersonal and political conflicts were advanced for their time. The true potentials of these profound concepts have not yet been fully exploited. India's as well as South Africa's independence processes are but the most preliminary success stories. In human civilization of the future perhaps many of the societal conflicts will be solved using Mahatma's methods.

I now suggest 'Shivagraha (Striving for Welfare)' and 'Sundaragraha (Striving for Beauty)' as further additions to this genre. We as modern day human beings will have to strive for the other two virtues as much as for the 'Striving for Truth' because Truth in isolation of the other two loses its relevance. The Truth is for whom, for what purpose?

The striving for welfare is the central force. It holds the other two strivings in an inseparable   98 triumvirate. If the welfare for a person can be ensured, the truths of her life can be upheld and her beauty enhanced. If she is not provided for, nor protected; neither her problems are solved, nor her aspirations are properly guided; where would she be? In other words Welfare (Shiva) alone stands for the four Ps (Providing, Protecting, Problem solving and Personal teaching) we discussed earlier. The truth and the beauty are no doubt important but not until and unless the basic nurturance is provided, the basic service is done.

We as human beings are in a curious position vis-à-vis God. Perhaps as a price of our superior intellect and material advancement we have lost our simplicity, our direct spiritual connection. Further, we have not been able to free our civilization from exploitation and destruction. We have removed ourselves far from Her proximity of truth, welfare and beauty.

Welfare therefore has to be the central concept for me, you, and others, the world. We as human beings will have to serve selflessly, if we are to reclaim our spiritual grounds. We have to serve ourselves, the fellow human beings and Nature that surrounds us. That is the spirit of 'Striving for Welfare'.

Striving for Beauty is important as well. Through hatred and discrimination we have created a lot of ugliness in today's world. God's creation is not beautiful to us anymore. We have tried hard to damage Mother Earth and to tarnish the image of an innocent human being. Both need to be accepted as a whole, healed, to be made handsome again.

Shivagraha and Sundaragraha are likely to be our guiding principles along with Satyagraha in the decades to come. You, as a modern person, are perhaps destined to be a volunteer for the welfare of humankind and the Universe.

You, I and other fellow beings will therefore achieve our respective places under the Sun if we continue to walk the path of 'Love Self and Love Others'. Love is one of the most important things in life, as an emotion, as a relationship and as an attitude. If we can care enough for ourselves, as well as for creation, do we need anything more, anything else for that matter?

Bibliography

American Psychiatric Association (1994): Diagnostic and Statistical Manual of Mental and Behavioural Disorders-4th edition (DSM-4). American Psychiatric Association, Washington DC.

Fischer L (1982): Gandhi: his life and message for the world. Penguin Group, New York.

Frankl V E (1970): Psychotherapy and existentialism, Souvenir Press, London.

Gambhirananda Swami (2000): Isa Upanisad, Advaita Ashrama, Calcutta.

Leff J and Vaughn C (1981): The role of maintenance therapy and relative expressed emotion in relapse of Schizophrenia: a two year follow up. British Journal of Psychiatry, 139, 102-4.

Maslow A H (1987): Motivation and personality. Longman, New York.

Rogers C A (2004): On becoming a person: a therapist's view of psychotherapy. Constable, London.

Shastry V and Pandey R K (2001): Manjul-Manjusha, Neeta Prakashan, New Delhi.

Surya N C (1993): Aham. Artworks, Hyderabad.

Lightning Source UK Ltd.
Milton Keynes UK
UKOW01f0956160617
303419UK00001B/110/P

9 780982 046777